PRISM OF THE HEART
A Spectrum of Life

BY
DARLA O'NEILL

TATE PUBLISHING, LLC

"Prism of the Heart" by Darla O'Neill

Copyright © 2005 by Darla O'Neill. All rights reserved.

Published in the United States of America
by Tate Publishing, LLC
127 East Trade Center Terrace
Mustang, OK 73064
(888) 361-9473

Book design copyright © 2005 by Tate Publishing, LLC. All rights reserved.

No part of this publication may be reproduced, stored in a retrieval system or transmitted in any way by any means, electronic, mechanical, photocopy, recording or otherwise without the prior permission of the author except as provided by USA copyright law.

All Scriptural references, unless otherwise stated, are taken from the *New American Standard Bible. All italics are added, for emphasis, by the author.*
Copyright: The Lockman Foundation, La Habra, California
1960, 1962, 1963, 1968, 1971, 1972, 1973
All rights reserved.

The Amplified Bible: Copyright: 1987 by the Zondervan Corporation and The Lockman Foundation. All rights reserved.

New Living Translation: Copyright: 1996 by Tyndale Charitable Trust. All rights reserved.

The Holy Bible: Authorized King James Version Copyright: 1999 by Holman Bible Publisher. All rights reserved.

ISBN: 1-9331482-2-5

This Book is Dedicated to . . .

each one whose heart is touched by these
stories, for *you* are the reason
they were written!

Table of Contents

Prologue 7
Author's Reflections. 9
Introduction 11
Heart Verses 13
A Faithful Friend 15
Ants 21
Battle Cry 31
Bondslave 37
Child of Grace. 43
Desert Song. 53
Heaven's Footprints. 59
Journey Into Love 65
Land of Degradation 83
Light Reflector 91
Man of Obedience 99
Portrait of Hypocrisy 105
Prayer Warrior 111
Reversal. 117
Sacrifice of Love 131
Sowing In Vain 141
Sword of Peace 145
The Accident. 157
The Doll. 163
The Puppet 167
The Toy Store 173
Touch of Love 181
Trademark of Evil 193
Words of Comfort. 199
Whosoever 207

Prologue

This book you now hold in your hands has been written with much prayer and a strong sense of God's leading, story by story, over the past twenty-five years. At the core, each story is an expression of deep convictions and insights in my own life through the experiences, struggles, joys, and heartaches that I have known. Yet I believe these stories go much deeper than just my own limited dimension of life on this earth.

Deep in my heart, throughout the years, has been a burning passion to express God's truths in a way that touches all of our lives, as followers of Jesus Christ—regardless of the multitude of distinctions that too often separate us from one another. On a human level, we are all "one flesh" for we are all descendents of our first human parents, Adam and Eve. As such, we all experience the same heart-felt longings and desires, strengths and weaknesses, virtues and sins that belong to the entire human race.

Yes, each one of us is a unique individual with a unique personality, background, experiences, and character traits. Yet there still remains a common bond that runs through each of our lives; a common bond that seeks after a meaningful purpose in living; a common bond that desires a reason to exist that is bigger and greater than we are as finite human beings; a common bond that seeks for the very meaning of life; that yearns to know, on a deeply personal level, the Creator, Savior, and Lord of all mankind. And there is a common bond, in all of us, that recognizes the seriousness with which the Eternal Righteous Judge evaluates our words and actions; indeed, the very thoughts and motives of our hearts (Matthew 12:6; Romans 2:1–8; II Corinthians 5:10; Hebrews 4:12).

In the end, after all is said and done, our lives are really about God. They are about the ways in which we, on earth, express or fail to express His love, compassion, forgiveness, patience, mercy and grace toward others, as well as the obedience, love and faith we express or fail to express toward Him. More than that, our lives are about the significant times and ways in which we humble ourselves before the Lord and allow Him to express Himself to us on a profoundly deep and personal, life-changing level. Those significant encounters with Him, and our responses to them, are what give life its sense of purpose and fulfillment. And such encounters may be directly with the Lord, Himself, or with Him through the life of some individual that He, strategically, places before us on life's pathway.

It is my earnest prayer, therefore, that as you read through the pages of this book, you will come to find expressed, in new and reflective ways, not just the grand prism of emotions and longings that comprise the human soul; not just the deep bond of oneness in the Lord that unites all true believers; but the one unchanging Constant in all of our lives . . . God Himself. Throughout the pages of this book, may you experience a new understanding of our Lord Jesus Christ and the great significance God places on each of our lives—both yours and mine—now and eternally!

Darla O'Neill
Holland, Michigan

Prism of My Heart

Before You, Lord, my heart does bow in gratefulness and praise,
thanking You for all the years of faithful love, displayed . . .
A spectrum fused with colors; life dimmed by hurt and pain,
Your loving hand, so gently touched the colors, to reclaim.

Thank You, Lord, for guiding me into Your dazzling light,
where colors, bright and pure, reflect the Prism of *Your* Life . . .
Forgiveness, love and mercy, compassion and Your grace;
colors of Your Being, no earthly hands create.
Colors clear, transparent, shining through earth's night;
colors washed in shades of red from Calvary's Sacrifice.

Thank You, Lord, for royal hues, midst suffering subdued
that I might know their brilliance, in dazzling magnitude . . .
Thank You for Your love that flowed, my sinful life to save.
Oh, may You see, in me, the living colors of pure praise!

Introduction

Like colors, bright and vivid, from a prism touched by light,
   our hearts reflect a spectrum, shining ever bright.
   Red—green—yellow—blue—orange—purple too,
 reflections of our feelings, our thoughts and attitudes:

Red for fiery passion and bloodied sacrifice,
 anguish, pain, and heartache;
 foundations of this life.

Green for tender longings of life's most wondrous joys,
 and greediness or envy; hypocrisy deployed.

Yellow for the cowardly, the timid and the weak,
 and intellectual mindset; worldly gains to seek.
 And for the joyful spirit, glowing bright with smiles
 of Victory, in the presence of those who would revile.

Blue for icy coldness, indifference or contempt;
 and lonely isolation, fears and discouragement.

Orange for warmth and goodness, the giving of oneself,
 and anger, in a righteous form; indignation felt.

Purple for a noble heart, tried and proven true,
 and courage with a trusting faith;
 great evils to subdue.

Colors—vivid colors—reflected by our lives,
brushed within our being; viewed by God's own eyes.

Colors—vivid colors—life or death impart,
judged by God eternally; the Prism of the Heart.

Heart Verses

"Teach me Your way, O Lord, that I may walk and live in Your truth; direct and unite my heart [solely, reverently] to fear and honor Your Name."

Psalm 86:11 (Amplified)

"Above all else, guard your heart, for it affects everything you do."

Proverbs 4:23 (NLT)

A FAITHFUL FRIEND

*Color me purple, orange, and yellow bright;
glimpse my heart, in loyalty delight.*

" *Love is patient and kind . . . Love does not demand its own way . . . Love never gives up . . . is always hopeful, and endures through every circumstance.*"

I Corinthians 13:4, 7 (NLT)

"A friend loves at all times . . ."

Proverbs 17:17a

I have a faithful, loyal friend who's very dear to me,
she's always there to count on when I'm tossed about Life's Sea.
For as strong waves of hurt and pain wash cruelly o'er my soul,
I sense my faithful, loyal friend gently soothe my woes.
Her eyes shine with compassion as she looks into my face,
and sympathy and kindness, her features softly trace.
No biting words of sharp retort ever cross her lips,
nor condescension's messenger—advice's lashing whip.
No verdict does she offer me for all my human wrongs,
nor does her heart e'er beat to any vain, self-righteous song,
but loyally defends me, despite my guilt and sin;
helping, in a gentle way, my victory to win.

She does not sit as Judge Supreme o'er secrets of my soul,
but offers me the kind of love that helps to make me whole.
No judgment do I sense from her by word or telltale nod,
for she would never dream of standing in the place of God.
Her comfort, gentle as it is, offers me sweet peace,
and helps, in some mysterious way, my soul to make release
of all my wretched sinfulness before God's righteous throne
where I, with all my thoughts and deeds,
      by Him am fully known.

And when, in joy, my heart breaks forth
      with happy songs of praise,
my friend is there beside me, her spirits quickly raised
by all the warmth and laughter reflected in my eyes,
a gift to her more precious than money e'er could buy!
She shares all my excitement in such openness and love,
I've never any doubt, at all, she's a gift from Heaven above;
sent to give me encouragement as I journey down life's road,
sent to give me comfort and help ease my heavy load,
sent to touch my lonely soul with strokes of God's deep care,
sent to softly whisper love, my every mood to share.

And when, through danger, I must pass
    with a trembling heart of fear,
my friend is there beside me to vanquish all my tears
for she has chosen to deem my life more precious than her own,
and thus, destruction's path she'll trod,
    despite the dangers known.
She'll gladly give her life for mine, if such must be the case
in hopes that by her own life's blood, the threat might be erased,
for when she chose to give her love, commitment was the cost,
and she'll pay the price, in full, despite what might be lost.

Oh, is it any wonder that I dearly love my friend
and strive to make her happy till she reaches journey's end?
And is it any wonder that her pains are real to me
or that her happy moods can set my heart at liberty?
And is it any wonder that she'll always have a part
of joyful, loving memories that are etched upon my heart? . . .
No, I doubt there be a man who firmly could deny
the power of such a loyal friend to draw me to her side.
And yet I now must tell you that this special friend from God
is just a lowly animal—my humble little dog!

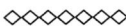

Oh, how often I have wished when thoughtless words lash me
that men who boast of all their love might,
    somehow, come to see
that points for loyal faithfulness and tender, loving care
are won more often by the dog, than men of pompous airs . . .
Oh, how that thought should shame us when we come to realize
how often we have failed the ones who on us do rely.
How often do our hearts condemn and fail to understand
the sorrows and the heartaches of our trusting fellow man?

How often do we utter words that made a weak soul cry,
and turn instead to find sweet peace in a friendly bark or sigh?

Think . . . oh think most clear, my friend,
          of the scene on Judgment Day
when men will stand before God's throne,
          their earthly deeds displayed.
All their good and mighty works will rise from earth's dark sod,
but tell me, will their works of love excel the faithful dog?
Will you and I be able, on that grand and fearful Day,
to stand before the Throne of God and confidently say
that loyalty and faithfulness our spirits have expressed
to those on earth who looked to us for comfort, love and rest?

Oh, how I fear that those who boast
          of mighty deeds they've done
will tremble when they stand, at last, before God's precious Son.
For as God's mighty scales are tipped by love . . . and love alone,
they'll find a tiny, humble dog, outweigh their good deeds, sown!

ANTS

*Color me orange, red, and purple;
glimpse my heart, compassionate and merciful.*

"Look at the heavens and see; and behold the clouds—they are higher than you. If you have sinned, what do you accomplish against Him? And if your transgressions are many, what do you do to Him? If you are righteous, what do you give to Him? Or what does He receive from your hand? Your wickedness is for a man like yourself, And your righteousness is for a son of man."

Job 35:5-8

The colony was busy on that early summer morn
as workers labored fervently, their talents proudly sworn
to finishing the Monument of tiny stones and dirt
erected by their efforts o'er two long months of work.
And happily, in confidence, they labored thus each day
knowing their reward, in praise and glory lay.
And as they worked, they sang this song, lifting voices high,
"All this for You, oh Mighty One, who towers o'er the sky.
We dedicate this Monument, created by our hands
to You—in deep devotion—oh great and noble Man."
And as they sang, their fellow ants shouted words of praise,
convincing them that all their work hadn't been in vain!

And not far from these workers labored other ants,
digging out a tunnel, their nest to e'er expand;
working, oh so earnestly, determined to create
a tunnel that would rival those other ants had made.
And as they worked they too did sing, lifting voices high,
"All this for You, oh Mighty One, who towers o'er the sky.
We dedicate this tunnel, created by our hands
to You—in deep devotion—oh great and noble Man."
And as they sang, their fellow ants shouted words of praise,
convincing them that all their work hadn't been in vain!

And from another tunnel came ants weighed down with food,
each one with a heavy load of particles, minute;
struggling with their burdens, bearing forth the crumbs
to place before the Monument . . . in tribute to that One.
And as they walked, they proudly sang, lifting voices high,
"All this for You, oh Mighty One, who towers o'er the sky.
We dedicate this bounty of food within our hands
to You—in deep devotion—oh great and noble Man."
And as they sang, their fellow ants shouted words of praise,
convincing them that all their work hadn't been in vain!

◇◇◇◇◇◇◇

Oh, how those ants thrived happily, midst all their busy work
knowing—to the Mighty One—each effort held great worth!
And how the ants took pleasure in speaking words of cheer
to all the zealous workers who proved their merit, clear.
And in honor of the leaders the ants proclaimed a day
for merriment and feasting with a banquet and parade.
Thus, proudly, were names mentioned of great and noble ants
who sacrificed all pleasure to aid the Cause of Man . . .
And tiny plaques of hardened dust were given as reward
to those who organized the work; their talents thus outpoured.
Designers of the Monument were given highest praise
with plaques that bore a blade of grass, an honor very great!
While builders of the tunnel, and donors of the food
received a simple plaque of dust, commending their tribute.

And though three of the builders
       complained about their plaques,
angry *they* had not received a valued blade of grass . . .
and a handful of the workers argued in disgust
that such a celebration really wasn't fair or just,
yet it was a big success, and all the ants agreed
that working for the Mighty One brought life's prosperity! . . .
And so they sang together, lifting voices high,
All thanks to You, oh Mighty One, who towers o'er the sky.
Glory and great honor You've placed within our hands;
reward for faithful service, to You, oh noble Man."
And as their voices blended in happy words of praise,
the ants rejoiced o'er all the fun of honoring Man's name!

◇◇◇◇◇◇◇

Autumn's golden colors now blazed in brilliant hues
and grassy fields were glistening in the early morning dew
when o'er the hill came Antman, a stranger in their midst,

greeting all around him with warmth and thoughtfulness.
A gentle ant and quiet, with unassuming ways,
but clearly not a worker, anxious for Man's praise . . .
And knowing that he didn't seek a valued plaque of dust,
the other ants regarded him with suspicion and distrust.
"He isn't really normal," the other ants all said.
"He's different from the rest of us, and surely is misled!"
Yes, they all decided, there was reason to beware
this strange, deceptive ant, their values not to share;
for while he spoke with kindness
      to their daughters and their sons,
he didn't praise the Monument, erected to that One.
And while he greeted, warmly, the workers—one and all,
their tunnel, dug so zealously, he never did applaud.
And no ant could remember hearing him express
appreciation to that One, conforming with the rest . . .
Clearly, he was lacking in devotion and in zeal,
an ant who failed, Man's noble name to honor and revere.
And so the ants all judged him, their wisdom to exert,
as one to warily regard . . . a poor inferior!

Twilight's glow was fading into the dark of night,
and multitudes of distant stars were twinkling in the sky
as Antman crossed the colony, quiet and alone,
lost in thoughts of noble Man, deep within his soul . . .
Oh, how he wished these ants could see
      that One for who He was,
instead of seeing only their achievements and status!
How he wished they understood that honor didn't rest
in plaques of dust or blades of grass or attendance at banquets,
for these were naught but recompense, ant extolling ant,
what value did these have before that great and mighty Man? . . .
Oh, thought Antman sadly, if these ants would only heed
the final verse of that great song, accepted as their creed.

And softly, in his gentle voice, he sang into the night,
"All praise to You, oh Mighty One, who towers o'er the sky.
I dedicate my life to You, and place within Your hands
all I am—as sacrifice—oh great and noble Man."
Reverently, he sang the verse, time and time again,
willing that the song go on, not wanting it to end . . .
And while no ants applauded him or shouted words of praise,
Antman felt a sense of joy . . . his weary spirits raised.

But suddenly through his song, he heard a frightened cry,
and turning 'round, he saw an ant lying on his side!
His legs were pulled up tightly, his body in pain, bent
as all alone, he struggled on the steps of the Monument.
"Help me," he cried weakly, sensing someone near,
and Antman reassured him whispering, *"Friend, I'm here."*
"I fell," the ant cried painfully. *"My feet slid off the stones*
up there on the Monument, despite my good foothold . . .
Oh, I know t'was folly to climb it with my crumbs;
my tribute to be placed, on top, before the Mighty One.
But I truly thought He'd honor me, more than all the rest
if I could only reach the top . . . my crumbs, there to present!

"And now," he cried in anguish, *"my body's bruised and sore*
and other ants will laugh at me, my folly to deplore!
Oh why . . . why did I slip on those stones, taking such a fall?
And why did Man not listen, not heed my desperate call?"
"Oh, my friend," Antman said, *"I'm sure He heard your cry,*
and while you may not understand, I know He has replied."
"Now lean on me and I will help you safely to your home,"
"and do not fear," he gently said, *"you won't be left alone."*
Slowly, through the darkness, the two ants struggled on,
sensing as they journeyed, a growing friendship bond.
And when they reached the tiny home of pebbles, dust, and dirt,
Antman laid his friend aside and quickly went to work.

First, he washed out all the wounds,
    and cleansed the gaping sores,
and then a healing ointment o'er
    his bleeding wounds, outpoured.
Next, he made a soothing drink with which to feed his friend,
giving him good nourishment, his body thus to mend.
And when the drink was finished, he rubbed his painful limbs,
restoring circulation lest any malfunction . . .
Finally, the ant relaxed in quietness and peace,
"Thank you," he said softly, as he drifted off to sleep.
*"You've been so very kind to me; you've done so much to help,
I never could have made it . . . struggling by myself."*
"And you know," he added thoughtfully,
    *"I've come to understand
the kindness and the sympathy that must be part of Man."*
A gentle smile crossed Antman's face, *"Yes,"* he softly said,
"Man is kind and good to us, heeding our distress."
And then he placed some valued crumbs, a generous supply,
beside his friend and turned, at last, bidding him goodnight.

The sun's warm rays touched Antman's face,
    arousing him from sleep
and anxiously, he left his home, his friend again to meet . . .
Quickly, over stones and dirt, he journeyed on his way;
greeting all around him, his friendliness conveyed.
And happily he thought of all the joy he'd come to know
in helping other fellow ants to bear their heavy loads . . .
Nothing he could e'er receive by words or deeds of praise
compared with helping others o'er their suffering and heartache.
And tiny plaques meant nothing, nor valued blades of grass
for Antman sought his treasure in kind and loving tasks! . . .

But suddenly all happy thoughts vanished from his mind
for Antman heard the rumble of angry shouts and cries.

And turning toward the Monument, he suddenly beheld
his friend receiving painful blows o'er raw and ugly welts!
Designers of the Monument and workers stood as one
lashing him for damage his painful fall had done . . .
for stones had tumbled to the ground and left a gaping hole
way up on the Monument all noble ants extolled.
And voices rang with anger, such folly to condemn
for no ant, worthy of Man's praise,
      dare show such vile contempt.
"Wicked ant!" they shouted, *"you've proved to us a foe!"*
And so the whip was raised, again, to strike another blow . . .
And then at last, their anger spent, the workers turned to leave,
returning to their work for Man; their noble, honored deeds!

Antman stood in silence, now alone beside his friend;
kindness and compassion, his presence to extend.
While in his heart he cried o'er all the cruelty and pain
inflicted on this fellow ant as Justice in Man's name! . . .
And as he slowly bent to touch the oozing, open sores,
his spirit grieved o'er all the pain this fellow ant had borne.
And looking at the Monument, he wondered in his soul
how ants could place such value upon mud and dirt and stones.

Oh, how he longed to show these ants that monuments of dirt
could never glorify that One, despite their zealous work.
And tunnels dug so earnestly and lauded with such praise
were worthless to that Mighty One
      and n'er could bless his name.
Nor could any sacrifice of choice and valued crumbs
earn for them a single word of tribute from that One!
For Man saw naught to honor in this great and complex nest;
a tiny mound of dirt within his mighty hand to rest.
And the greatest ant this colony could boast before that Man
could not, by his own effort, a single eyelash span! . . .
Oh, how very foolish these ants were to believe

that from themselves, the Mighty One, a blessing could receive;
that for their goodly efforts and highly lauded work,
the Mighty One would honor them and magnify their dirt;
that tiny stones slipped from their hold and fallen to the ground
could justify the lashing whip, its sharp and crackling sound!

Gently now with tenderness, Antman held his friend
and carried him, e'er lovingly, support and help to lend,
while fighting back painful tears, he once more raised his voice
to sing, again, the thoughtful words o'er which his soul rejoiced.
And so he sang with shaking voice, tears glistening his eyes,
*"All praise to You, oh Mighty One who towers o'er the sky.
I dedicate my life to You, and place within Your hands
all I am—as sacrifice—oh great and noble Man."*

Then suddenly before him the path of dirt and dust
changed into a surface, soft and smooth to touch.
And as he journeyed down that path, he marveled o'er the sense
that what his small feet walked upon was blissfully immense!
And Antman felt a lightness his body had never known
as now he left behind him all dirt and dust and stones . . .
And then a mighty awesome wind blew o'er his tiny form
as that surface lifted . . . into the sky, airborne!

And suddenly, with wonder and all-consuming awe,
Antman looked into the face of a giant human god!
And then he knew, that surface, unlike the stony land,
was a human, fleshly finger, upon the hand of Man!

And now he heard the Mighty Voice echo o'er the sky,
*"Well done, my friend, I honor you for all your sacrifice.
Come now into the ANTHILL prepared for honored ants,
and feast o'er all the bounty in its wide and vast expanse!"*
And so as Antman and his friend held onto Man, secured,
that Mighty One arose, and toward the ANTHILL turned.

And gazing o'er Man's finger . . . far, far below,
Antman saw the colony; a tiny heap of stones . . .
And suddenly that Mighty Man, through the silence hushed,
stepped . . . and by his might foot, that colony was crushed!

BATTLE CRY

 *Color me red, green and blue;*
glimpse my heart, with evil imbued.

"Little children, let no one deceive you; the one who practices righteousness is righteous, just as He is righteous . . . By this the children of God and the children of the devil are obvious: any one who does not practice righteousness is not of God, nor the one who does not love his brother. For this is the message which you have heard from the beginning, that we should love one another . . . We know that we have passed out of death into life, because we love the brethren. He who does not love abides in death."

I John 3: 7, 10–11, 14

*F*ar down the dusty road they came that sunlit afternoon,
twelve hundred soldiers marching brave into the face of doom.
For they had heard and answered firm their country's battle cry;
the call for men of valor to fight and bleed and die!
And as they marched, they sang this song
      with voices deep and true;
"We go to conquer evil, corruptness to uproot.
We go to carry righteousness to all men, far and near,
to guarantee our children the freedom from all fear."

The crowd that lined the road that day
      cheered the proud men on,
and joined them in happy heart to sing the Conquerors' Song.
And three men marching out in front waved the swastika high,
for like the rest they, too, were proud to be on Hitler's side!

Oh, how we scorn and mock these men for atrocious evil done,
and yet we too, who call on God, the Devil's course may run.
We fight to conquer evil with spirits brave and true,
and yet somehow, it's evil with which evil we pursue . . .
Clothed in moral goodness, convinced of being right,
we call on God to sanction deeds abhorrent in his sight!
We march about the church today, in godly raiment, fair
forgetting Satan is, himself, clothed with pious airs.
We hide all of our wretchedness behind a moral mask,
and point at others 'round us who've been tarnished in the task
of living life as God above has chosen to ordain;
walking in a manner worthy of his name.
We search for all the wickedness in others we can find
and then sit down at the Judgment Table, lavishly to dine.
We chew on sin-sweet morsels of gossip that supply
the poisons that our spirits crave to give us peace of mind.
For like a strong and powerful drug
      that numbs man's sense of pain,

these tempting morsels numb us from our sense of moral stain.

And so we jab at this one, give another a vicious blow
and slap the sinner about the church until he's filled with woe.
We stand as executioners of the judgments of our God,
and thus, our brothers and sisters, with his Holy Word we flog!
And when, at last, they turn away in heartfelt sorrow and pain,
we shake our heads, e'er knowingly,
      o'er how they've dishonored the faith.
Then laying down our spiritual whip
      with a prayerful, godly, touch,
we thank the Lord for his glorious Word . . .
      and all his redeeming love!

Far down the dusty road they came that sunlit afternoon,
two thousand years ago they marched into the face of doom
for they had heard and answered firm religions' battle cry;
to vanquish those who blasphemed God, and openly denied
their rituals and sacred rules; writs of God's command,
rules that made one worthy . . . a godly, righteous man! . . .
They wore long robes that marked them
      as distinguished men of God
and prided themselves on keeping every word of Mosaic Law.
They did no evil, like common men, purity was on their side,
and thus all wretched sinners, they fiercely did decry.
None were so religious as these staunchly righteous men
and none were more determined in searching out all sin!
Loudly, they denounced all evil they could clearly see
and prided themselves on all their goodness and moral purity.
And as they marched, they sang this song
      with voices deep and true;
"We go to conquer evil, corruptness to uproot.
We go to carry righteousness to all men, far and near,
to guarantee our children the freedom from all fear."

The crowd that lined the road that day
        cheered the proud men on,
and joined them in happy heart to sing the Conquerors' Song.
For they were going to crucify a plague upon the world;
a Man who scorned their rituals; denouncing their good works!

He did not fit their pattern of religious morality,
for He openly talked with sinners of God's love for humanity.
Prostitutes and swindlers, He said He came to save
and even the most despicable ones, He freely forgave!
A woman taken in adultery, He refused to stone or denounce
while with one phrase, her accusers, He very swiftly oust.
He did not point his finger at the wretchedness of men,
instead, He spoke of salvation . . . secured by faith in Him.
He claimed that rules and rituals weren't part of salvation's plan,
and even the most unorthodox could walk with God,
        hand in hand! . . .
To the Samaritan woman at Jacob's Well,
He shared forth God's love, not visions of Hell.
He spoke of believers who know God, in heart,
regardless of doctrines that religion imparts.
He spoke of Heaven's Water, poured forth evermore,
to quench thirsty souls, be they outcasts and whores . . .
No amount of righteous deeds could pay sin's awesome price.
For man's redemption, blood alone, was the proper sacrifice.
And He, the spotless Lamb of God, would pay that price in full
that of Gods' matchless love and mercy, man might fully know!

"Blasphemy!" cried out the angry moralists that day.
"Your life reflects just evil in the way You do behave!
You surely have a demon; we know 'tis plainly true,
for God will surely honor us for keeping all his rules!
And all the vile, lost sinners who seek Jehovah now,
must join with this group of ours . . . evil to cast out!"
And so they crucified that Man upon a wooden cross,

all the time, not knowing, that they were truly lost . . .
All the time believing that their deed was just and grand
and won for them a higher place in Heaven's holy land!

⋄⋄⋄⋄⋄⋄⋄

Today, as modern moralists abuse their brothers, cruel,
may they stop and ponder Gods' supremely guiding Rule.
He said that Love was worth far more than all our sacrifice,
and that, unless we live it, no efforts will suffice
to win us God's approval and bring us safely Home
to his side, in Glory, and a seat before his throne . . .
For God is love, completely;
    compassionate through and through,
and if we are to reflect his Spirit,
    we must be compassionate too!
Humble and gentle, loving and kind,
the Master drew sinners to walk by his side.
And with tenderness great, but with grasp most firm,
He discipled the lowly; God's mercy discerned.

Oh, may we remember when pride hovers near
that to our Lord, each soul is most dear . . .
And no word or deed to Him is unknown,
be it whispered in secret, or in darkness sown!
The least of our brothers and sisters on earth,
in his sight, is valued at infinite worth! . . .
And so it behooves those called by his name
to share forth his love on the human plane;
to share his compassion with suffering hearts,
his mercy and grace, to each one impart . . .
And when judgment enters our souls, once again,
may understanding, to our souls, be sent.
For when we abuse those for whom He died,
we are really abusing Him, on High!

BONDSLAVE

*Color me purple, bright yellow, and orange;
glimpse my heart, love's triumph adorned.*

> "... Behold, the bondslave of the Lord; be it done unto me according to your word."
>
> **Luke 1:38**

She was a bondslave . . . belonging to Another,
and yet within that bondage, freedom ever hovered.
For bondage was not cruelly forced upon her soul,
t'was given by her freely; her spirit in control.
She chose to be a servant, bending forth her will;
complying with the wishes Another did instill.

And so . . .
She journeyed down a path of pain and heartache great,
accepting all the hurtful turns her tender life did take.

She was a bondslave . . . and so she gave up dreams
of wealth and worldly pleasures; status to achieve.
She gave up dreams of owning great and valued things
in exchange for service, a priceless gift to bring.
She gave up dreams of luxuries, a soft and carefree life,
choosing to outpour herself . . . a living sacrifice.
She had few things of value, nothing to possess.
If her Master asked for them, she'd honor his request.
She valued all the qualities that men so often shun;
humility and kindness, through loving actions, done.

And so . . .
The dazzling riches and pleasures of this life
never touched her humble soul, distractions to entice.

She was a bondslave . . . and so she bore a Child,
labeled illegitimate, by others e'er reviled.
Those who saw and knew her . . . neighbors, even friends,
gossiped o'er her shameful act; held her in contempt.

And voices cruelly whispered down the narrow, dusty streets,
proclaiming forth her folly, her shame to e'er repeat. . . .
Parents warned their daughters not to be deceived;
"This girl," they said, *"most certainly,*
        God's judgment will e'er reap!"

Thus o'er her life, a stigma, forevermore held true
among those who had watched her grow
                from childhood into youth.

She was a bondslave . . . and so she left her home
to journey to a foreign land of strangers e'er unknown.
She lived among a people she could not understand,
thankful for a place to rest; obscure within that land.
Asking naught but solitude, a shelter warm, secure;
a place where three could safely dwell
                from wrath and hate, unfurled.

And so . . .
She raised her little Child, midst strangers all around,
thankful for the quiet peace within that vast land, found.

She was a bondslave . . . and so she came, once more,
to live within the country in which she had been born.
And with her Child and husband, she settled once again
within her own home town, midst relatives and friends.
And there she watched her small Child
                grow into a strong young man;
authority and power, his life to e'er command.
She watched as men were drawn to follow at his side,
calling Him their Master; their lives to sacrifice.

And she watched as men with hatred, deep within their souls
rose up against her Son, his life to overthrow.
People she had known throughout her childhood years,
now arose in one accord, her Son to mock and jeer . . .
And then with bitter anger, their hatred cruelly fed,
she watched those very people seek to put her Son to death!
But walking through their midst, He journeyed on his way,
heading toward his destiny . . . a large and wooden stake.

She was a bondslave . . . and so she came, at last,
to stand before a wooden cross on which her Son held fast.
She stood and watched his precious life ebbing fast away
and thought of all the promises she'd heard God's angel say.
"You shall bear a Son," said Gabriel, to her sent,
"and of his mighty Kingdom, there shall be no end."
But now her Son was dying, tortured and in pain;
was all her loving sacrifice forever wrought in vain?
Had her Master failed her and left her all alone;
the depths of bitter heartache and agony to know?

Helplessly, she watched as spikes
      were driven through his hands,
and thought of how she'd held them within that foreign land.
She saw the sponge of vinegar raised to touch his lips
and thought of how she'd nursed Him . . . nourishment to give.
And when a soldier raised a spear and pierced his precious side,
she felt a pain within her heart no words could e'er describe.
"A sword shall pierce your own soul," Simeon had said,
and now those words were ringing, loud within her head . . .
But then through all her heartache,
      she heard her Son's dear voice,
lovingly committing her to the disciple of his choice.
And from that very hour, she went into John's home,
because her Son had spoken . . . and his will was now her own.

And so . . .
Through all the heartache of that dark and awesome Day,
hope still kindled deep within; God's will she still obeyed . . .

She was a bondslave . . . and so on Resurrection Morn,
great joy replaced her sorrow o'er the Son that she had borne!
And she, too, was a believer within the Upper Room;
God's promises fulfilled in Jesus' triumph o'er the tomb . . .

All the words she'd treasured in her heart, so long ago
were proven true, as God's great love now flooded o'er her soul!

And so . . .
Her voice was raised in prayers and praise to God above,
proving love's devotion . . . the Master e'er to laud.
For she was just a servant, seeking forth God's will;
seeking by her humbled life, his purpose to fulfill . . .
And thus, her heart sang joyfully with worship evermore,
for her precious, cherished Son, became her Risen Lord!

And Mary said:

"My soul exalts the Lord, and my spirit has rejoiced in God my Savior. For He has had regard for the humble state of His bondslave; For behold, from this time on all generations will count me blessed. For the Mighty One has done great things for me; and holy is His name."

Luke 1: 46–49

CHILD OF GRACE

Color me purple, tender green and bright yellow; glimpse my heart, devoted and loyal.

The Law says . . .

"When the Lord your God shall bring you into the land where you are entering to possess it, and shall clear away many nations before you . . . and when the Lord your God shall deliver them before you . . . then you shall utterly destroy them. You shall make no covenant with them and show no favor to them. Furthermore, you shall not intermarry with them: you shall not give your daughters to their sons, nor shall you take their daughters for your sons."

Deuteronomy 7: 1- 3

Author's Note:

This story, although based on Scripture, is fictional and is not intended to accurately interpret the Biblical account. However, after studying the Old Testament record, I think it is possible—and perhaps even probable—that events occurred in just this way . . .

He first beheld her beauty in the early morning sun
as gracefully she crossed the fields, the harvest just begun.
And o'er his strong and handsome face, a trace of love did glow
as cautiously she looked his way, a gentle smile bestowed. . . .
Truly, he had never seen a girl so beautiful,
           one who, inexplicably, touched his very soul.
And somewhere deep within him there stirred the lost belief
that God's own plan prepared for him a very special "Eve."
"Look there," he called out softly to the friend along his side,
"who's that girl with long dark hair, over to the right?"

"A stranger," came the answer in a mocking undertone,
"a daughter of the Gentiles; a blemish midst our own.
A sinner, I am certain, who has come into our land
to bring about the ruin of our men of noble rank;
seducing them to evil, no doubt, with kindly smiles,
charming them toward wicked deeds; their bodies to defile.
True, she has been welcomed for deeds of goodness done.
But how could she . . . a Gentile . . . e'er bless the Holy One?
And what befalls our nation if our purity's outpoured
by welcoming into our midst such wretched, sinful whores?"

Silently, the two men walked down the dusty road,
lost in thoughts e'er springing from
           the depths of their own souls.
And one man thought of purity; the Laws of God above,
while the other thought about the wonder of God's love.
One man thought of Judgment toward all the Gentiles, lost;
vengeance reaped, upon the ones, God's wisdom never sought.
While mercy and forgiveness filled the other man
with praise for his Jehovah . . . his open, outstretched hands.
And one thought of obedience; the Law to guard his steps,
while the other thought, with shame, of his own sinfulness.
And one, now, saw the other as straying from God's truth

and sought, with words of warning, such folly to rebuke.
"Remember," he said sternly, *"sin paves destruction's end!"*
"I know," the other answered, *"remember, too, my friend!"*

◇◇◇◇◇◇

Daily, now he watched for her to enter his own fields;
gleaning from the bounty the harvest time e'er yields.
And when at last, he saw her, deep joy his spirit marked
with the sense she'd now come home
                to his own land . . . and heart.
Thus eagerly, he crossed his fields, determined now to know
this girl who seemed a vision to tantalize his soul.

And in his deep and manly voice, he bid a warm *"Shalom,"*
greeting her e'er kindly as she stood there, all alone.
"May our God be with you," he very gently said.
"May He bless my lord," she answered, bowing low her head.
And o'er her face, he clearly saw a deepening blush arise.
No, he thought, she is not one, Jehovah to despise! . . .
"I bid you stay within my fields until the harvest is done;
glean among my reapers, my servants, and their sons.
Drink the water drawn forth by the younger lads,
and join with my reapers for the afternoon repast."

Humbly now she bowed her head as tears rose in her eyes,
"My lord is very gracious," she thoughtfully replied.
"For I am but a foreigner, a beggar on your land;
far below your servants, such kindness to command!
And how is it my lord does show such mercy unto me,
one so undeserving . . . of your notice unworthy?"
Looking up into his face, she saw a handsome smile
and thought of noble women his charm could e'er beguile.
And in her heart she marveled that such a mighty man
would even dare to speak with her upon his fertile land.

For she had little merit, no wealth or noble birth,
and yet he spoke as if she were a woman of great worth!

"I know," he said, *"you risked your life to save two of our own;
believing in the Holy One your people have not known.
And thus you stand as worthy as any Israelite
to share in all the bounty that Jehovah did provide."*
"Yet in truth," he gently said, turning now to go,
"none of us are worthy of God's blessings e'er bestowed!"

◇◇◇◇◇◇◇

O'er the weeks of harvest, she labored now each day
within the fields of this great man, his kindness e'er displayed.
And never did she suffer from the want she'd known before;
never did she hunger or thirst for substance, more.
And never did she sense, again, the scorn and deep contempt
that followed her from field to field, where e'er in need she went.
For in this time of harvest, she reaped far more than grain;
she reaped respect from this great man, e'er calling her by name.
And others who had scorned her soon came to realize
that even she . . . a Gentile . . . was not to be despised!

But then, one day, as sunset's glow
              dimmed faintly 'cross the sky,
she journeyed home not knowing, two men her footsteps, spied.
And suddenly they grabbed her and forced her to the ground,
brutal hands defiling her, not knowing any bounds;
ripping at her clothing, bruising sore her limbs,
calling her obscenities, chafing rough her skin;
silencing her desperate cries with sweaty, grimy hands;
crushing her thin body 'neath their heavy, muscled span. . . .

"Oh God!" she prayed in terror, *"save me . . . oh my God!"*
And suddenly, in answer, both men sprawled on the sod;
quivering with terror, like animals in fright

as o'er them loomed a mighty man, holding forth their lives!
Swiftly, in his anger, he fought them both at once,
fists like granite smashing them, despite their anguished grunts;
battering their faces till both men cried in pain
and tunics, soaked with rancid sweat,
        showed sticky reddish stains. . . .
"Spare us!" they cried desperately, *"spare us . . . oh my lord!"*
as on the ground, their bodies squirmed in painful anguish, sore.
And then, at last, they heard him speak
        o'er their heaving breaths . . .
"Go," he said, *"but n'er return, unless you seek for death!"*
And stumbling in their anguish, the two men swiftly ran,
fearing lest this mighty lord their lives would still demand!

◇◇◇◇◇◇◇

Stars were glistening faintly in the early evening sky
and birds were softly singing their carols to the night
as o'er the fields of harvest there walked a Gentile girl,
her face aglow with loving trust for her gallant protector.
But in her heart, she pondered o'er words of hurt and pain;
words she knew she had to speak, protecting his good name.

"Oh, my lord," she said at last, *"it has fully been a week*
since that night . . . in mercy . . . you came to rescue me.
Please my lord, I beg you, cease to walk me home;
it is enough you rescued me, no debt to me you owe!"

Silently, he gazed at her, amusement on his face.
"No," he said, *"I owe no debt . . . but your debt, you mistake!"*
"Surely," he said boldly, *"the rescuer has claims*
upon the one he rescues and from destruction saves.
And surely, do you owe me a large, substantial sum."
"So how," he said teasingly,
        "shall you repay my kindness, done?"
But suddenly to his surprise, the girl grew very still;

color draining from her face as o'er her eyes tears spilled.
"No!" she said in a trembling voice, running from his side
as if pursued by demons, exposing their disguise.
And cursing at the folly of his thoughtless, teasing words,
the man now turned and swiftly ran . . . pursuing after her,
until at last, he caught her and pulled her to a stop.
"No!" he said breathlessly, *"it isn't what you thought!"*

But heedlessly she answered . . . staring up at him,
"I know," she said, *"men view me as an object fit for sin.*
But though I am a Gentile, from a people e'er defiled,
Jehovah has redeemed me and made me his own child.
And He has e'er forgiven me for evil I have done;
sinful deeds I had to do to save my precious ones.
For my brothers and my sisters, and my feeble parents, too,
would have starved within that land were I not a prostitute!"

"I know," the man now answered in a kind and tender voice,
"but truly, you do wrong me if you think, with you, I toy!
For by Jehovah's loving grace, no Israelite could know
salvation any greater than, on you, He has bestowed.
And as Jehovah reigns o'er me, the Master of my life,
I tell you now, in truth . . . my love . . . I seek you for my wife;
the one to share my earthly days, to walk this land with me,
to share in all the blessings that Jehovah gives, so free.
And never shall you know, again, such bitterness and shame,
for you shall stand beside me, bearing forth my name.
And as a noble woman, honored from her birth,
so shall you . . . my precious love . . .
          be deemed of equal worth!"
"Oh, my lord!" she answered now, in wonderment and awe,
fighting back the threatening tears of disbelief . . . and love.
"You . . . you cannot mean . . ." the words arose
          and touched upon her lips,
"I do!" he said, and silenced her, gently, with a kiss.

◇◇◇◇◇◇

And o'er their love, God's blessing was mightily outpoured,
for from this lowly, Gentile girl, a noble child was born.
And through the years, he grew to be a valiant man of God;
master, as his father was, o'er fields of harvest, lush . . .
And then one sunlit morning, when fields were rich with grain,
a poor and lowly stranger, into his bounty came.
And glancing o'er the golden fields, he suddenly beheld
this foreign girl . . . a Gentile . . . from a people e'er defiled.
"Look there," he called out softly to the servant by his side,
"who's that girl with long dark hair, over to the right?"
"A Moabite," the answer came, *"a foreigner named Ruth."*
"Yes," Boaz answered, *"deep inside . . . I knew!"*

And as he walked across his fields to greet this humble girl,
somewhere deep within him, his mother's voice he heard.
*"Though I am a Gentile, from a people e'er defiled,
Jehovah has redeemed me and made me his own child."*
And looking down upon Ruth's face, he came to understand
the kinship of two strangers within God's gracious plan.
For like his precious mother, this girl now stood in need
of someone strong and honored, her substance to redeem;
someone who would understand the value of her life,
despite the fact she wasn't born a chosen Israelite;
someone who would see in her Jehovah's loving grace
and o'er her humble being, his redeeming mercy trace.
Someone who would care for her . . . a woman of great worth;
valued not for beauty's charm, but spiritual rebirth.

And somewhere now within him, Boaz clearly sensed
the longing, as Ruth's Someone, his protection to extend.
For hearing of her virtues, he knew her noble heart
was filled with deep devotion for God's goodness and regard.
And standing now beside her, he sensed within his soul

a place where his protection, o'er Ruth, could e'er unfold.
For looking deep within her eyes, he saw reflected clear,
her purity of spirit . . . Jehovah to revere.
And looking deep within her eyes, he saw reflected back
the loving trust his father saw . . . years ago . . . in his Rahab.

God's Grace says . . .

" . . . Rahab the harlot and all who are with her in the house shall live, because she hid the messengers . . ."

Joshua 6: 17b

"And to Salmon was born Boaz by Rahab; and to Boaz was born Obed by Ruth; and to Obed, Jesse; and to Jesse was born David, the King."

Matthew 1: 5 - 6

DESERT SONG

Color me red, blue and yellow bright;
glimpse my heart, it's desperate plight.

"The afflicted and needy are seeking water, but there is none, and their tongue is parched with thirst; I, the LORD, will answer them Myself, as the God of Israel I will not forsake them."

Isaiah 41: 17

𝒢round was shifting violently underneath my feet,
surging up to meet me in the cruel, relentless heat
as beads of perspiration glistened on my skin;
rivulets of water, my eyes and mouth to rim.
And o'er my form a scorching wind ceaselessly did blow;
blasts of fiery passion that left me clammy, cold;
helpless e'er to fight against my stomach's churning force,
to stop the waves of nausea that o'er my body coursed.
Helpless to resist within my feeble, finite shell,
nature's searing fury . . . all human strength dispelled.
Helpless . . . now exhausted . . . my legs no more to stand;
     Falling . . .
         falling helplessly . . .
             my lips to taste of sand.

Silently I lay upon the blanket of the earth,
feeling naught but burning heat and unrelenting thirst;
hearing deep within me, the whispered call of death,
knowing now it's presence, my very breath caressed.
And in my heart, I prayed that God would let me swiftly die,
"Please!" I cried out hoarsely, tears scalding in my eyes.
       "Please . . .
          please . . .
             please!"
I cried out desperately, pounding slippery fists
into sand that covered me . . . a hot and powdery mist.
But Death's black cloak of darkness faltered o'er my soul
as a hand of might and power, it's conquest did withhold!

Then opening my burning eyes, I saw a dazzling scene;
a turquoise lake of water, beautiful, serene!
And o'er that scorching desert, I felt life touch my skin,
fingers wet with cooling hope, stroking deep within.
Slowly, with a labored breath, I rose from off the sand,

straining . . . now determined . . . to reach that blessed land;
marveling o'er the miracle provided by my God
to save me from destruction, the desert's hapless lot.
Marveling that, in mercy, God granted unto me
a source of life and healing for full recovery,
certain of salvation provided by that lake,
seeing in its presence, God's mighty Hand of Fate . . .
And knowing in my throbbing heart, the battle was not lost,
my spirit rose triumphant, that sparkling lake to laud!

But to my growing horror and anguished disbelief,
the lake grew ever fainter, a vision in retreat;
mocking at my confidence, laughing at my faith;
shouting that my trust in God had been a big mistake!
For water e'er eluded me, defied my desperate grasp
as sand slid through my fingers; the bitter drink of death.
And what had seemed a miracle of mercy from my God
I knew, at last, was nothing but the desert's cruel mirage!

Blackness flooded o'er me as I fell upon my knees,
beyond the point of thinking, vanquished in defeat.
All hope now truly gone as I closed my burning eyes;
past the point of caring, past the urge to cry.
Death had won the battle, had triumphed o'er my soul,
and now would claim it's victory and clasp me in its hold!
And so as sand blew o'er me, a Celebration Feat,
I waited for the Conqueror; my spirit to concede.

But then I heard the footsteps echo 'cross the sand;
walking ever closer . . . footsteps of a Man.
And suddenly I felt it; water on my lips,
precious, priceless water, my burning thirst to quench!
Water . . . water . . . water . . . coursing down my throat,
pouring through my body; my withered flesh to soak!
Water . . . precious water . . . cool and crystal clear,

sent by God, in triumph, o'er the desert's fiery bier!
But water far more precious than any from earth's lakes,
flowing from a Mighty Source I never could mistake.
For as my eyes with wonder, beheld the loving Man,
I saw that I was drinking from
      his cupped and nail-scarred hands!

Author's Note:

Many years ago, I read a relatively unknown poem that had been printed in an article of a local newspaper. Over the years since then, that poem has become increasingly popular and is, today, widely recognized as the much loved Christian classic, "Footprints." My story, "Heaven's Footprints," was written shortly after I first read that poem and was, indeed, inspired by its compelling message.

HEAVEN'S FOOTPRINTS

Color me orange, blue and tender green;
glimpse my heart, love's companionship seen.

> "The Lord . . . raiseth up the poor out of the dust, and lifteth up the beggar from the dunghill . . . for the pillars of the earth are the LORD's, and He hath set the world upon them. He will keep the feet of His saint . . ."
>
> **I Samuel 2: 7–9 (KJV)**

Walking Life's Shore ~

I walked along the ocean's shore one misty afternoon
and dug my bare feet deeply into the sandy dunes
as ocean waves broke gently o'er my ankles and my feet
and carried back my footprints into the rushing sea.

No trace of my existence remained upon the shore
for either friend or stranger to know I'd gone before.
And yet I knew, so clearly, the path I had just trod,
and knew that every footprint was recorded by my God.

And so it did not matter that my presence was unknown,
or that my prints upon the shore were not in permanence sown.
For God, in his vast Heaven, a cast had carefully made
of each and every footprint upon the shore I'd laid . . .
And so as waves with rushing force erased my finite steps,
I turned my eyes toward Heaven's Shore where God,
      each print, has kept.

> "He brought me up out of the pit of destruction, out of the miry clay; and He set my feet upon a rock making my footsteps firm."
>
> **Psalm 40: 2**

Knowing Life's Lord ~

I walked along the ocean's shore one misty afternoon
and dug my bare feet deeply into the sandy dunes
as ocean waves broke gently o'er my ankles and my feet
and carried back my footsteps into the rushing sea.

Then suddenly ahead of me I spied upon the beach
a set of perfect footprints where the ocean could not reach.
And sensing in my heart great joy, I hurried forth to stand
with my feet now resting on the footprints of the Man's.

Slowly and most awkwardly, I journeyed down the shore,
stepping ever carefully into those prints that bore
a mark of pain and suffering that I came to understand;
a round and gaping hole where a nail had pierced the sand.
And as I walked, I marveled o'er the warmth that I could feel
washing o'er my body as my feet touched toe to heel
with those awesome footprints of which there seemed no end,
stretching out before me, beckoning as a friend,
asking me to make the marks footprints of my own,
to journey in those awesome steps until I reached my Home.

But as my heart cried, *"Yes, I will,"* in answer to that call,
I sensed the mighty ocean . . . in fury . . . rise and fall,
and crash against the seashore in an effort to erase
every human footprint of which there was a trace!
But all in vain, it stretched its arms up toward the dampened sod

where I now journeyed, safely Home, step in step with God.
And all in vain, it beat its waves against the battered shore,
for in my Lord, no waves could touch my footprints, anymore!

"If I should say, 'My foot has slipped,' Thy lovingkindness, O LORD, will hold me up."

Psalm 94:18

"Like a shepherd He will tend His flock, in His arm He will gather the lambs, and carry them in His bosom."

Isaiah 40: 11

Bearing Life's Storms ~

I walked along the ocean's shore one misty afternoon
and dug my bare feet deeply into the sandy dunes
as ocean waves broke gently o'er the vast and sparkling shore
where, all alone, I stood beside the footprints of my Lord.

For many years we'd journeyed thus, my precious Lord and me,
o'er the finite sands of time, on toward eternity.
But now I sensed life's journey coming quickly to an end,
and lost in deep and troubled thought,
     I pondered o'er my Friend.
For as I stood and gazed upon the shore we long had trod,
I found one set of footprints often missing from the sod.

There before my vision, etched upon the sand,
were places where, in solitude, I seemed alone to stand;
places where I clearly had been left to walk alone,
to fight life's cruelest battles in a strength that was my own.
For where life's pains and sorrows had lashed my aching soul,
I found one set of footprints, alone, to bear the load.
And so my heart with anger accused my loving Friend,
"You said that You'd go with me until the very end.

*You said You'd never leave me
       even through the roughest storms,
but always give me comfort, in Your Presence, safe and warm.
But as I gaze behind me o'er the path through life I've trod,
I find that I have often been deserted by my God!"*

Then through my tears I felt my Friend gently touch my hand,
"Oh, my child," He softly said, *"you do not understand.
For I have never left you as you've journeyed down this way,
nor have I ever failed you or your confidence betrayed.
Look close at those lone footprints
       that are etched upon earth's sod,
and you will find, my precious child, that they belong to God.
For when strong waves of sorrow beat cruelly o'er your soul,
I carried you within My arms, and bore their fury, full."*

JOURNEY INTO LOVE

Color me blue, red and orange;
glimpse my heart, compassion borne.

"If I speak with the tongues of men and of angels, but do not have love, I have become a noisy gong or a clanging cymbal. And if I have the gift of prophecy, and know all mysteries and all knowledge; and if I have all faith, so as to remove mountains, but do not have love, I am nothing. And if I give all my possessions to feed the poor, and if I deliver my body to be burned, but do not have love, it profits me nothing."

I Corinthians 13: 1–3

"Beloved, let us love one another, for love is from God; and every one who loves is born of God and knows God. The one who does not love does not know God, for God is love."

I John 4: 7–8

*F*orty years have come and gone since that fateful day
and my hair has slowly turned from black to shades of gray.
But as my earthly life is drawing quickly to a close,
the memory of that fateful day is etched upon my soul.
For on that day so many long and distant years ago,
my heart did quail with terror and my spirit filled with woe,
for all my grand illusions, with force, came crashing down
as I saw most clearly the path where I was bound.
Of that Day of Reckoning my soul shall n'er forget
for God, in his great mercy, Satan's strategy upset.
And God, in his great love, the Counterfeiter did dethrone
as Satan stood before my eyes, his presence fully known.
Oh, my friend, please listen to the words I share with you
if you seek to follow God and not be Satan's tool.
And if you truly seek to serve our Lord with all your heart,
please, oh please, heed the truths I seek now to impart!

⋄⋄⋄⋄⋄⋄⋄

That day was warm and sunny and birds sang in the trees,
for Spring was coming early to our small community.
And vividly I now recall, as if t'were yesterday,
the daffodils and roses that I spied upon my way
as I walked along the steep and narrow dusty road,
pondering o'er my duties and the large and heavy load
of work that lay before me in the church I pastored here,
where I sought to lead God's flock in reverence and fear.

So young and so devoted to the service of my God,
I sensed his special favor as the dusty road I trod,
for in my zeal and fervency, I ever sought to share
all the mighty Truths of God with those under my care.
And with my life devoted to honoring his Name,
I ever sought, before the lost, his standards to proclaim.
Always so determined to live wholly for my Lord,

I sacrificed all earthly wealth for Heaven's treasures, stored,
and always turned in horror from all pleasures known to man
that could, in any way, deter me from God's strict commands!
Oh, I was very righteous and godly in those days,
and lived as an example for all those who'd gone astray;
pointing to the folly of their wickedness and sin,
seeking by my pious life, their Hell-bound souls to win . . .
And so that sunny morning, with all confidence, serene,
I walked into my office and greeted Bobby Scheen.

Now Bobby was a quiet lad, a boy just twenty-one
with large and homely features and dull eyes of deepest brown.
Orphaned from an early age, he lived his life alone,
with just a few possessions in a shack that he called home.
And no one ever bothered to make of him a friend,
for he was not the kind of lad with which one cared to spend,
time that could be given to helping other folk
who followed God's Commandments
      by deeds and words they spoke.

Oh, Bobby was a Christian, at least that's what he'd say,
but every now and then, he would regress to sinful ways
and assume, again, the habits that very clearly showed
that down the Road to Glory, he still had a ways to go!
And so intent on helping him to reach God's Standards, high,
I met with him each week as a counselor and guide,
leading him in study of God's holy, divine Word;
hoping that his footsteps on sin's path might be deterred . . .
But all my strident efforts seemed now to be in vain,
for in his life, no change could I clearly ascertain.
And so that fateful morning, as I sat behind my desk,
I pondered o'er the best way to issue my request
that of these weekly meetings we make a clear-cut end
for nothing left me more upset than time unwisely spent!
Oh, Bobby was a nice young lad, of that I had no doubt,

but spiritual development was what I cared about.
And sensing now his failure to grow up in the Lord,
I felt my efforts wasted and my time, in vain, outpoured.
So in my kindest manner, I gently did explain
just why these weekly meetings were a bother and a strain.

But as I spoke, I sensed the boy grow rigid and quite still,
and suddenly I saw large tears o'er his dark eyes spill . . .
"You're just like all the rest," he cried in anger and despair,
"about me, as a person, you've never really cared!
You only gave your time in the hopes that I would be
before God's throne, your shining and impressive trophy;
a bright and sparkling jewel to wear within your crown
when before God's presence, you stand on Heaven's ground.
Well, I'm sorry if I've failed you and taken up your time;
I'm sure someone more promising, you easily will find . . .
And with our weekly meetings, you needn't bother anymore,
for never will I, once again, cross your office door!"

For a long and silent moment, tension filled the air
as sad and lonely eyes into my own did boldly stare.
And then before I knew it, I stood there all alone
for Bobby, from my office, like a bird of prey had flown!

Shaking my head, sadly, I sensed a deep dismay
that in so poor a manner Bobby Scheen could behave.
And now I knew for certain that my feelings were correct,
for godly folk would ne'er toward me display such disrespect!
No, Bobby had not grown in the knowledge of our Lord,
else such vile behavior he would clearly have abhorred.
And so with satisfaction and a deep sense of relief,
I focused all my thoughts on the things I could achieve
with the extra hour, each week, I now could claim
in which to serve my precious Lord and glorify his name . . .
Bobby had just wasted my short and valued time,

and so with peace and comfort, I dismissed him from my mind.

◇◇◇◇◇◇◇

The office clock had just struck four that fateful afternoon
when through my mind there flashed, somehow,
      the sense of pending doom.
And even to this day, I still can hear the phone's sharp ring
as knowledge of the tragedy, to me, a friend did bring . . .
The train was traveling, rapidly, down the narrow tracks
when suddenly there was a sharp and horrible impact
as a young and quiet lad . . . nobler than he seemed,
was crushed beneath the mighty wheels
      while people yelled and screamed!
Yes, Bobby was the one who lost his earthly life that day
and traded pauper's rags for Heaven's robes of grand array.
And two small little boys have grown
      to manhood o'er these years
for Bobby pushed them off the tracks,
      else their limbs were sheared.
Yes, Bobby was the one who made that noble sacrifice
while others . . . far more 'godly' . . . held on safely to their lives
and watched the scene unfolding from positions where no harm
could possibly have caused them any personal alarm!

I sat in silence, shaken, as the story did unfold
and thought of Bobby's sacrifice, so very brave and bold . . .
But suddenly, deep horror filled the chambers of my heart
at the awesome news my friend did now impart,
for one of those small children, but for Bobby overrun,
was none other than Jonathan, my dear and precious son!

As I journeyed home that night, down the sun-lit road,
I crossed large fields of sweet and fragrant yellow marigolds.
And birds were singing softly, in the green leaves of the trees
as Spring's mild wind brushed o'er my face,

   a calm and gentle breeze.
But none of these things mattered as I walked along the sod,
for I was holding, in my heart, communion with my God,
thanking Him for mercy that saved my own dear boy,
despite the fact that Bobby's earthly life had been destroyed.
And sensing in my spirit, God's omnipotent control
o'er a situation that, with terror, filled my soul,
I raised my voice toward Heaven in earnest, heartfelt praise
and thanked God for the gracious love,
   toward me, He did display!
But somehow, for a reason that I did not understand,
I sensed my prayer just echo back across the distant land.

◇◇◇◇◇◇

That night I tossed with nightmares, restless on my bed
and suddenly awoke to a frightening sense of dread,
for somewhere in the darkness of that still and eerie room,
I heard a lad's voice call to me beyond death's earthly tomb.
"You never cared at all, for me," Bobby's voice intoned,
*"nor did your life, to me, reflect the love of God, made known.
I thought that, of all people, you would care about my soul,
but all you ever cared about was reaching your fine goals!"*

Then suddenly across the room, I saw dark glowing eyes
focus on my face . . . my soul to terrify!
And frightened in the darkness, my heart did palpitate
for the look of deep reproach, I never could mistake!
"Even in my death," the haunting voice continued on,
*"you sense no grief or sorrow o'er my earthly presence, gone.
But in your heart, you think that God had shown special grace,
by saving your dear Jonathan while my life was erased."*
Then all at once those pensive eyes faded from my view
as the haunting spirit from my presence withdrew.
And once more night's dread stillness, my straining ears assailed
with nothing but the singing of a lonely nightingale.

Restlessly, I rose from bed, unable more to sleep
for my mind, in turmoil, spun with fearful anguish, deep.
And seeking some escape from the night's appalling scene,
I fled into the brisk night air, in the hopes of sweeping clean
the thoughts that so disturbed me in the depths of my own soul
and left me with confusion and a fearful sense of woe.
But so vivid were those haunting eyes that stared into my face,
that even on the dusty road, my form they still embraced.
And while the night air gently cooled my hot and burning skin,
my mind continued, restlessly, in feverish dread to spin.

◇◇◇◇◇◇◇

Then suddenly before me, the road was filled with light
as I saw a man approach whose form was glistening white!
And taking my hand, boldly, he called me by my name
and said that God had sent him in the hopes that I would gain
an understanding spirit in the knowledge of the Lord;
a heart discerning insight of *true* spiritual rewards.
He said that God had sent him, my errors to reveal;
to show me all the folly of my fervency and zeal
in the hopes that as I listened to God's holy divine Word,
my footsteps, on sin's pathway, might clearly be deterred.
Then beckoning me to follow, down a narrow rocky lane,
slowly we descended to a hellish, black domain.

At first I could see nothing save the man's own dazzling light,
but slowly, as we journeyed on, I once more gained my sight.
And to my eyes, there rose a scene so horrible and vile,
that my most frightening nightmares, by comparison, were mild.
Even to this day, I still shudder to recall
the horrors that I spied upon that hellish cavern, sprawled.
And ever in my nostrils, I can smell the putrid stench
that rose from all the filth with which
          the cavern had been drenched.
Nor could I e'er forget the sound ringing in my ears

of people's anguished wails, as if they burned on fiery biers.
Yet destined in this torment, ever to remain,
they gnashed their teeth and screamed aloud
      a blasphemous refrain.
And were I not protected by God's holy shining Light,
I knew that I would be insane e'er morning dawned from night,
for n'er could I escape the truth I knew so very well,
that God, by His own messenger, had taken me to Hell!

"This is the Canyon of the Damned," my guide did now explain,
"where those who walked in earthly pride,
      forever, are enchained.
Ruling their souls proudly with disdain for their God,
they chose, by their heart attitude, this place to ever trod.
And God takes no delight or joy in their presence here,
but at his grace and matchless love, they haughtily did sneer.
And scorning an eternal home in Heaven's Paradise,
they sought this Pit of Darkness in which to agonize
and curse the Name, forever, of the God who rules all men
and had the power to save them from the folly of their sins."

Then pointing to the multitude that writhed with torment, deep,
my guide continued to explain the way this Hell was reaped.
"God does not seek destruction for the sons of men," he said,
"for it was for their sakes, alone, Christ suffered painful death.
He came to earth, a Sacrifice, that they might ever live
with Him who loved them dearly, and their sins did all forgive.
But spurning his great love, they chose
      to live their earthly days
pursuing earthly pleasures in a proud and selfish way.
And some lived lives of wickedness, debauchery, and sin,
while others sought, by righteous deeds,
      God's favor thus to win.
Some, ruled by carnal passions, after fleshly goals did strive,
while other hearts were driven by the force of righteous pride.

*And some had dreams of living all life's pleasures to the full,
while others, just like Satan, had high and lofty goals,
and sought to stand in Heaven by a power all their own;
to boast in all the works, that by their own hands,
    they had sown.
But Heaven is not merited by righteous actions, done.
It cannot be attained by those who spurn God's precious Son.
And as the sons of men are viewed
    from God's great throne above,
His Spirit seeks the hearts of those reflecting forth his love."*

Then farther down the putrid pit my guide did lead me on
until we came to stand beside a fiery, fetid pond
where multitudes of people sought
    to quench their burning thirst,
as with vile words of hatred, God's holy name they cursed.
And glancing o'er the multitude, I came to understand
why my guide had called this pit the Canyon of the Damned.
For even though their bodies burned with hellish fire, sore,
not one was heard to cry aloud in pity for the Lord.
No voice was raised in anguish for compassion or God's grace,
nor was there any sorrow to be found on any face.
But in a strange and eerie way, they joined with one accord
to scream aloud their hatred for the One they all abhorred.
And as a mighty army, that revels in its sin,
they praised the name of Satan and owned him as their King!

Oh, how my heart did tremble as I viewed those vile, lost men,
and how very fervently, I thanked the Lord, again,
that of their tragic destiny, I n'er would have a part,
for God had truly saved my soul,
    and ransomed forth my heart! . . .
But then I sensed his messenger stirring by my side
and I knew my thoughts had been revealed to this, my guide.
For now with gentle pressure, he led me down the path

to stand before a sinner who had tasted of God's wrath.
And suddenly my soul was filled with terror all anew,
for this wicked, vile, lost sinner had been my good friend, Hugh!

Never had I known a man, in speech more eloquent,
preaching forth the Gospel where'er in life he went.
Devoted to the cause of God with fervency and zeal,
he ever sought to share God's truths; his judgments to reveal.
A swayer of vast multitudes, he moved men everywhere
with a voice like angels' song upon the open air.
And people came from miles around
      to hear him speak God's Word;
to listen to this mighty and magnificent orator! . . .
Oh, n'er could I imagine how this scalding pit of Hell
had come to be the final place in which his soul did dwell.
For Hugh was all the preacher that I ever dreamed to be;
the man who spurred within my heart respect and jealousy!

Then I heard God's messenger give answer to my thoughts
and explain, most clearly, just why Hugh's soul was lost.
"This man," he said, *"sought his reward*
      in terms of earthly praise
and now must dwell within the depths of Hell's eternal blaze.
For while his lips did utter forth great words of holy truth,
his heart did seek the praise of man from early days of youth.
And while his speech, on earth, did bring
      man's praise and loud applause,
God found nothing, in his heart, to honor or to laud.
For all his thoughts were focused on achieving worldly fame;
on building for himself, on earth, a grand and glorious name.
And in his heart was found no love for God or any man,
but just a haughty attitude, his spirit did command.
And so when life was ended and eternity begun,
he found himself in darkness, far removed from God's dear Son,
for Paradise can be a home for naught but humbled souls

who have tasted of God's mercy, and by love,
    have been made whole."

Then slowly down the rocky path we journeyed, once again
until with shock I spied, once more, an old departed friend.
And in a state of disbelief, I stared into his face
and pondered how he, too, did now inhabit such a place!
Pastor Sam, I thought, had been among God's Choice Elect
for never, in my father's church, had one had more respect!
A gifted man of prophesy, he spoke God's message, clear,
and set young souls e'er trembling with reverence and fear.

And as the preacher's son, I still can hear my father say
that Sam must have a wealthy crown, in Heaven, laid away!
For God had truly granted him a knowledge of his Word,
and by his guiding counsel, souls from sin were oft deterred.
So how did such a godly man fail to find God's grace;
failed upon his earthly death,
    to pass through Heaven's gates? . . .
And how could I have hope of ever reaching Paradise
if God did shun Sam's efforts and ignore his sacrifice?

Then once again, God's messenger gave answer to my thoughts
and explained, most clearly, just why Sam's soul was lost.
"This man," he said, *"possessed great gifts*
    of faith and prophesy,
but in his heart, they spurred a sense of superiority.
And while he sought to minister those gifts in God's own Name,
his heart did beat a proud and very arrogant refrain.
Many weak and trusting souls, who on him did depend,
were shattered e'er his lofty pride, their spirits did offend.
For judging other people by a standard all his own,
he praised the ones who followed him,
    by righteous actions, sown.
And like the mighty Pharisees, who lived so long ago,

all those who failed to please him, he haughtily opposed.
Pity and compassion n'er were found within his heart,
but just self-righteous arrogance, his spirit did impart.
And so his mighty efforts to please the Lord, above,
all burn within Hell's fire, devoid of any love."

Standing there in silence, I pondered all these things
and thought of love's great value before the Lord and King.
For godly deeds of righteousness, however great or small,
devoid of love, did find an end o'er Hell's great cavern sprawled.
And when a man departs from earth
      to stand before God's throne,
it seems that what God cares about is love . . . and love alone.
And all man's gifts and talents, no matter what they be,
devoid of love, will merit just a hellish destiny!

Then farther down the rocky road, again we made our way
over flowing rivers of unspeakable decay.
And trembling in my heart with fear, I dared not raise my eyes
at the sight of earthly men, in Hell, dehumanized.
But fervently I prayed to God this journey soon would end,
as my guide said gently, *"You must visit one more friend."*
And hearing eerie footsteps, I turned around to see
another man approaching from this Pit of Agony . . .
Vividly, I still recall the look upon his face;
a vile and wretched horror, his features clearly traced.
And barely did I recognize this man I once had known,
who cursed the Name of Jesus
      with such loud and wretched groans.
Oh, how my soul did tremble, and my heart with terror quake,
as slowly he approached me from out a burning lake.
For all that I remembered about my good friend, John,
seemed completely foreign to this fiend from Hell, beyond!

John had been a pious man whose earthly life was spent

in leading others in their quest for spiritual development.
And he was my example, my counselor and guide;
the man on whose advice I always did rely
for none seemed more devoted to reaching all the lost,
despite the personal sacrifice, and great financial cost.
And none were more self-giving of all they did possess
in the hopes that others, by such giving would be blessed.
Oh, John seemed so devoted to honoring God's Name,
that clearly did I vote him to the Christian Hall of Fame!
And when his life was ended on a foreign mission field,
I felt all Heaven's glories were, to him, fully revealed . . .
Oh, how could I imagine that this Hell would be his lot;
that his deeds of righteousness, in Hell, would burn and rot?
And if my friend did merit Hell upon his earthly death,
then how could I, his follower, merit Heaven's best? . . .
And how could I find favor before God's holy throne
when John found naught but Hell in which
      to agonize and groan!?

Then once again, God's messenger gave answer to my thoughts
and explained, most clearly, just why John's soul was lost.
"This man," he said, *"gave all he had in order to achieve*
before the saints in Heaven, a position of authority.
He sought to be the greatest among the sons of men;
to stand before God's Presence, a royal crown to win.
But all his earthly sacrifice was ever wrought in vain
for, without love, he never could glorify God's Name.
And like so many others, seeking Heaven by good works,
he found, behind his actions, satanic forces lurked.
For all man's high ambitions, however justified,
at their core, reveal a heart of selfishness and pride.
And while he called on Jesus as his Master and his Lord,
his heart, by arrogance and pride,
      that precious Name, abhorred.
For ever seeking, selfishly, his own goals to fulfill,

*he never found the time on earth to seek God's perfect will.
And so . . . in truth . . . he never sought God's Name to magnify,
but just a place of prominence before God's throne on High.
And love was never found to have a place within his heart
as God's truths, to others, he labored to impart."*

◇◇◇◇◇◇◇

Then as I tried, in silence, these words to understand,
I felt my guide reach out and take a firm grip on my hand.
And suddenly o'er my face, the cool night air did blow
as once more, beneath my feet, I found the country road . . .
A thousand stars did glitter in the black and endless sky
as to my ears arose, again, the nightingale's sweet cry.
And n'er was life more precious, more valuable and dear,
nor was I ever happier to stand upon earth's sphere!
And tears did glisten in my eyes, as on my knees I fell,
praying that the Lord above would save *my* soul from Hell;
praying for God's mercy, no matter what the cost,
that unlike all the others, *my* soul would not be lost!

And then with shock, I saw him, still standing by my side;
the messenger whom God had sent, through Hell to be my guide!
And as his bright and dazzling form did slowly disappear,
these words I heard him utter with a voice quite firm and clear.
*"God truly takes no pleasure in the loss of any soul
but seeks, by lovingkindness, all men to be made whole.
And with pity and compassion does his Spirit e'er embrace
all of his creation, born into the human race.
But those who shun his Spirit, like the angels who once fell,
will find themselves, forever, cast into the Pit of Hell.
For it is not enough to simply call on Him as Lord;
one must have, within his heart, the love of the Savior.
And without love, it matters not how much one may achieve
or whether one acknowledges, in Jesus, a belief
for even Satan's demons, who burn within Hell's flames,*

tremble in belief o'er the precious Savior's Name . . .
So if you would see Heaven when your days on earth are done,
seek above all else to have the Spirit of God's Son;
to love with his compassion, to minister his grace;
to help the poor and needy, who on earth have been displaced.
And put aside all lofty dreams of power and prestige,
for God cannot honor those who seek such to achieve! . . .
And n'er forget the blessed truth that Jesus came to die
for boys, like Bobby Scheen, who on earth are so despised.
For every soul is valued by the God who reigns above;
who seeks to ransom every man by his mercy and his love.
And how you view the lowly and despised upon the earth,
is how, in truth, you view the God
        who gives each man his birth . . .
So if the weak and lowly, in spirit, you condemn,
you will not find God's favor before the sons of men.
And if from you, the lowly find naught but judgment, stern,
then how can you expect to find God's love and mercy earned?
Oh, do not be deceived by those, who righteous deeds extol,
while their hearts, toward God and man, remain quite
        hard and cold.
For only those reflecting forth the love of God's dear Son
will find, at death, God's favor and Heaven's glories, won."

Then suddenly I stood there, in the darkness, all alone,
trembling o'er the knowledge of all I'd just been shown;
praying that the Lord would fill my heart with his great love,
that I might, truly, represent His Son who reigns above! . . .
And as I prayed, I sensed God grant my troubled soul release
and fill my heart with love, and a deep sense of his peace.
And softly did I hear his voice whisper in my soul,
"I send you now to tend My lambs and bear the orphans' load."

◇◇◇◇◇◇◇

You asked me how I came to found this orphanage for boys,

a place that radiates forth love and deep abiding joy;
where each lad is thought special in his own and unique way,
a precious gift from God to brighten all our earthly days . . .
Well, now you know the story, my dear and special friend,
of why, within this Home for Boys, my earthly life's been spent.
And you know just why my eyes did glisten bright with tears
when you asked about the boy whose picture hangs in here.
For forty years have come and gone since that fateful day
when Bobby Scheen lost his life that others he might save.
But n'er could I forget the boy who looked to me for love
when all I had to offer was a self-righteous rebuff . . .
And n'er could I forget the look of pain upon his face
as from my presence . . . stern, unkind . . . he rapidly did race
out into the countryside, all alone to cry,
near the place where, shortly, he was called upon to die.

Now my life grows weary and my eyes are dimmed with age,
and one day, soon, I'll bid farewell upon earth's transient stage
as Heaven's gates are opened to admit my timeless soul
into the Realm of Glory where God's Presence I'll behold! . . .
And many of my loved ones, I'll greet with tears of joy,
but all the while, my eyes will scan the crowd for one dear boy.
And if the Lord should grant, that day,
         my heart's most cherished dream,
I'll view all Heaven's splendors, side by side, with Bobby Scheen!

LAND OF DEGRADATION

*Color me yellow, blue and red;
glimpse my heart, it's fearful dread.*

"For Jerusalem has stumbled, and Judah has fallen, because their speech and their actions are against the LORD, to rebel against His glorious presence. . . . Moreover, the LORD said, 'Because the daughters of Zion are proud, and walk with heads held high . . . Therefore the Lord will afflict the scalp of the daughters of Zion with scabs, and the LORD will make their foreheads bare. . . . Now it will come about that instead of sweet perfume there will be putrefaction; instead of a belt, a rope; instead of well-set hair, a plucked-out scalp; instead of fine clothes, a donning of sackcloth; and branding instead of beauty. . . . So the common man will be humbled, and the man of importance abased, the eyes of the proud also will be abased.'"

Isaiah 3: 8, 16–17, 24, 5:15

"*L*ast night I had the strangest dream I've had in many years,
t'was that rich and hearty meal before bedtime, I fear
that gave me such a nightmare, sweeping o'er my mind
with visions that will haunt my soul
              for quite some length of time."
"Oh, come now," Margaret lightly said, passing me a roll,
"dreams are naught but phantasm; reality opposed.
Surely, you aren't frightened by imagination's ghosts;
specters that your mind conceives . . . figmentary foes?"
"Oh, no," I quickly answered, smiling at my guest,
"but still this dream was vivid, more distinct than all the rest."
Margaret sighed and brushed a crumb from off the tablecloth
as I poured more coffee from the sterling silver pot.
And then she sat back leisurely in the velvet chair,
ready now to listen to all I had to share.
"So tell me all about it," she very sweetly said;
a dignified and courteous social thoroughbred.

"Well," I answered slowly, "t'was some strange and eerie place
where all lines of distinction clearly were erased."
"How ghastly!" Margaret whispered, stroking her soft furs.
"Oh, yes," I firmly answered, "t'was a nightmare, that's for sure!
For n'er could I imagine a curse so very cruel
as being numbered in the lot of common knaves and fools.
And n'er could I imagine a more horrid, ghastly fate
than all the lines of culture to e'er eradicate!"

"No," said Margaret thoughtfully, smoothing her silk dress,
"such a dream could, easily, leave one quite depressed."
"Oh, yes," I answered fervently, "for how could we e'er stand
in such a bleak and horribly indiscriminate land?
How could you or I survive in such an awful place,
forced to stand as equal to the lowly and debased? . . .
And how could we be known as women of noble birth

without all our possessions . . . distinctions of our worth?"
"How, indeed," Margaret said, and smiled up at my face;
a woman so well-mannered, of unerring poise and grace.
"Well what, exactly, did you dream?" my friend politely asked,
sipping at her sherry in a long-stemmed crystal glass.

"Well," I said, *"it clearly was some dark and desolate land
where multitudes of people, in numbered groups did stand.
And everyone wore the same ghastly uniform,
and to oppressive, stringent rules, everyone conformed.
Yet each one stood alone, fighting to survive
o'er some awesome terror that threatened all their lives . . .
Children, men, and women were exploited, all the same,
regardless of their rank, affluence, or their name.
And all were forced to labor, as abused and tortured slaves
'till death, their bodies decomposed within an earthly grave."*

"Oh, Margaret," I said fiercely, as chills ran up my spine,
*"death with life, throughout this land, did always intertwine.
For sickness and disease, starvation, freezing cold,
swept the land of people . . . an awesome, frightening toll!
And those who did survive, be they kings or imbeciles,
were mutilated viciously, tortured cruel, and killed
by people e'er envenomed with bitterness and hate;
vipers filled with poison, in a human form and shape . . .
And in my dream, I saw myself standing, side by side,
with all those nameless people who were destined, thus to die!
I found myself e'er clothed in that ghastly uniform
as dawn to dusk, I labored*
        *o'er some wretched job, performed . . .
And thus, I stood with people from every walk of life,
with lowly maids and butlers, with tradesmen and housewives.
I stood beside the outcasts . . . the dregs from off the earth;
crude and common peasants of ignominious birth.
And all the pain and anguish encountered in that land*

I, too, was forced to suffer by some tyrant's cruel command.
And none could e'er deliver me from such a horrid place,
filled with living corpses . . . atrocious human waste!
For none were found to care about the highborn or elite;
none were found to give a thought o'er my nobility! . . .
And all my vast possessions, my title and my wealth
could not buy a crust of bread with which to feed myself!
For all men sought to save their lives, devoid of all concern
o'er such noble beings . . . by wealth, their status earned.
And nothing was of value in that bleak and awful land,
except each man's endurance; death's call to e'er withstand.
And yet t'was not a single thing that any man could do
to grant him death's reprieve e'er his numbered lot they drew,
for t'was no value placed upon any human life,
and all men stood as equals . . . hatefully despised!"

"Oh, Margaret," I now muttered, as the vision swept my mind;
a kaleidoscope of savagery e'er forced upon mankind.
"N'er could you imagine the disgrace and horrid shame
I felt by being so reviled, treated inhumane.
For I was ever looked upon with hatred and contempt
and n'er from any suffering or pain was I exempt . . .
Prostitutes and rogues, the scum from off the earth
labored e'er beside me and scorned my rank and worth!
And all of us were ever viewed by some unseen foe
as cattle fit for slaughter . . . no . . . no . . ."
"flies," I whispered hoarsely, *"we were looked upon as flies,*
just dirty little insects to smash and pulverize.
For on this barren landscape, a fire ever blazed;
searing flames of brilliance; a cindery, grayish haze.
And putrid clouds of smoke e'er billowed through the air;
grimy ashes o'er the land . . . of skin and bones and hair!"

"Julia," came the soothing voice, calling now my name;
calmly beckoning me back from that hellish domain . . .

"My dear," she said so sweetly, patting my stiff arm,
smiling reassuringly, effusing gracious charm.
*"T'was just a wretched nightmare, your mind to domineer
within that slumberous realm; imagination's sphere.
For where on all the earth could you encounter such a scene?
Where could life's reality e'er merge with such a dream?"*
And suddenly she laughed aloud, as if it were a joke;
the absence of a fire, midst thick and billowy smoke . . .
And sensing the absurdity of such a hellish place,
I, too, now laughed as reality, my nightmare did erase!

Then sitting back in my chair, I smoothed my own silk dress,
and spoke of more aesthetic things with this, my special guest.
Gaily now, we chatted . . . pleasantries exchanged
as from my mind did fade the dream
      by which I'd been enchained.
From my mind, that nightmare and pending sense of doom
vanished as I glanced about the richly furnished room.
For all my vast possessions in my large, expansive home
fully gave the lie to that nightmare I'd bemoaned!
And Margaret's warmth and friendliness,
      my spirit gently calmed,
silencing completely, my apprehensive qualms . . .
And so we spoke of many things of interest to us both;
possessions we accrued, people we did loathe.
We spoke of awesome world events; the changing of the times,
of hungry, desperate people and a rising rate of crime . . .

But then my friend exclaimed o'er a man whose voice was heard
sweeping o'er our Country . . . men's souls, his doctrine stirred.
"You know," she said, *"I truly sense some awesome destiny
touching all the world through this man in Germany."*
"Oh, Julia," she exclaimed, *" he's marvelous, so superb,
I'm certain that he, soon, will be this Country's new Fuhrer!"*
"Impassioned and dynamic, he's what our Country needs

to lift us from this wretched curse of obscurity!"
"Perhaps," I slowly answered, "but his doctrines e'er imbue
citizens of Germany with hatred for the Jews."
"Nonsense," came my friend's reply,
    "there's nothing we should fear,
we are Germans, after all . . . loyal and sincere.
And thus, we stand with all the rest,
    despite our race and creed."
"Oh, Julia," she said fervently, "don't fear such bigotry!"

And then she sweetly smiled at me as if I were a child,
ignorant and foolish, by fantasies beguiled.
"Don't worry, dear," she gently said, pulling on her furs,
"all of us will prosper e'er this man becomes Fuhrer!"
"Yes," I answered slowly, "I . . . I'm sure that you are right;
perhaps, 'tis now the time to reform the German Reich . . .
Perhaps this man will bring us prestige and world acclaim,
for Germany, too long, has been ignored; its worth disdained!"

"Yes," she answered firmly, now kissing me good-bye;
her warmth and sweet affection, my fears to all belie.
And sensing all her confidence, so readily assumed,
I silently decried my foolish sense of doom.
For I was e'er the pessimist . . . the doubting, fearful one
whose somber thoughts produced a dull and ever gray spectrum.
I was e'er the one to color all reality
in dingy, tarnished hues; a drab facsimile! . . .
And so I firmly chided my apprehensive thoughts,
for I was, too, a German . . . a loyal patriot!
And from my mind, anxiety, its doubts and fears, did flee
for I was, after all, of German aristocracy . . .

"Oh, Julia," I exclaimed in the depths of my own soul,
"why are you so foolish, such horrid thoughts condoned?
Why are you e'er chasing dark shadows through the night;

glimpsing ghastly horrors . . . your spirit to affright?
Why must you e'er focus on monsters, yet unseen;
reality e'er tainted by some cruel nightmarish dream?"
And so I made a fervent vow, forevermore to see
just the pleasant, happy aspects of reality! . . .
And then with all my fearful qualms e'er subdued, at last,
I thought about that silly dream
                            and laughed
                                      and laughed
                                                  and laughed.

LIGHT REFLECTOR

*Color me orange, red and purple;
glimpse my heart, proven true and faithful.*

"Let your light so shine before men that they may see your moral excellence and your praiseworthy, noble, and good deeds and recognize and honor and praise and glorify your Father Who is in Heaven."

Matthew 5:16 (Amplified)

"*I'm a Christian,*" I announced as silence filled the air
and five men turned 'round swiftly, at my face to boldly stare.
"*A what?*" they asked. "*You're joking! . . .
       a Christian, did you say;
one of those fanatics who talk of God and pray?*"
And then they laughed and jeered at me in their mocking scorn
as if I were a funny freak with large crossed eyes and horns! . . .
And one man mocked me louder than any of the rest
for Peter hated Christians, their doctrine to detest.
"*Don't be a fool,*" he laughed and jeered, "*for everybody knows
that Christians are a freaky lot; a bunch of strange weirdoes!*"
"*Don't you have more brains than that?*"
       his mocking voice intoned,
"*don't you have more character, more guts, and firm backbone?
For all that Christian garbage is nothing but a crutch,
to help those poor 'ol weaklings
       whose spirits have been crushed!*"

"*I'm sorry that you feel that way,*" I truthfully replied,
"*but Jesus came to earth for me, and for my sins He died.
And what I tell you now, my friend, is the honest truth,
that when He died to save my soul . . . He also died for you!*"
Peter turned and glared at me, hatred in his eyes,
then he gave an angry grunt and walked off from my side.
Quickly, all the other four followed in his steps,
and so I found myself alone, as silence o'er me crept.

But then I thought of Jesus, and wondered how He felt
when He hung upon the cross, by all mankind repelled.
I wondered what went through his mind on that awesome day
when all his friends deserted Him, their confidence betrayed.
And somehow, thoughts of Jesus softened all my hurt,
for I had suffered nothing of the pain that He endured!

◇◇◇◇◇◇◇

True to my expectations, things grew from bad to worse
as those men now shunned me at the office where we worked.
And swiftly, I became the butt of all their dirty jokes
as incessantly, they sought my anger to provoke.
"How's it going, Christian?" Peter often jeered,
"fitted yet for that crown you'll wear in Heaven's Sphere?
"Come on," he'd say, "just loosen up . . .
    carouse and drink and swear.
Don't be such a kill-joy; such a pious, pompous square!"
Surely, for a little fun, your soul won't be condemned.
"But" he laughed, "on second thought,
    your crown might lose a gem!"

Then he'd blow smoke in my face from his cigarette
and leisurely stroll back, once more, to his office desk,
while people 'round the room would laugh
    and firmly shake their heads;
thinking he was funny, agreeing with all he'd said.
And I would sit and grit my teeth as anger in me flamed
o'er the way he mocked me and my precious Savior's Name!

But then I thought of Jesus, suffering man's abuse;
fingers pointing at Him, by sinful men accused.
Yet standing e'er in silence, speaking not a word;
the Sacrificial Lamb of God . . . Heaven's Arbiter . . .
knowing all authority rested in his hands,
yet for man's salvation, all blame to e'er withstand.
And somehow, thoughts of Jesus softened all my hurt,
for I had suffered nothing of the pain that He endured!

◇◇◇◇◇◇◇

Then one day the mocking took a cruel and ugly form
as people gossiped, viciously; integrity to scorn.
For now around the office, there spread a nasty lie;
whispers passed from here to there, by hatred fortified.
They said that I, a single man, living with a friend

did, in fact, live the sort of life God's Word condemns.
People turned and stared at me as if they understood
the reason I had values considered to be good . . .
They said that I was wholesome, not morally impure
because no normal feelings were found for any girl!
Temptation was unknown within my heart they said,
for no man who was normal, such desires could have fled.
And one man sneered more loudly than any of the rest
for Peter ever sought my life, by hatred, to oppress.
"Oh, God," I cried out bitterly, deep within my soul,
"may You vindicate my life before my hateful foes!"

But then I thought of Jesus, reviled and mocked and scorned;
considered illegitimate from the day that He was born.
I wondered what men said about the Savior, Jesus Christ
who had no human children or adoring earthly wife!
I wondered what they said about God's pure and spotless Son
who traveled with a group of men until his martyrdom . . .
I wondered what they called Him
     when compassion He e'er showed
by healing men, with a touch; God's mercy e'er bestowed.
And somehow, thoughts of Jesus softened all my hurt,
for I had suffered nothing of the pain that He endured!

◇◇◇◇◇◇◇

I was sitting at my office desk, working busily
when suddenly I smelled the smoke that o'er the office seeped.
And rising from my chair with a deep sense of alarm,
I quickly turned toward my boss and grabbed him by the arm.
"There's a fire, Sam!" I whispered, and quickly he arose;
heading for the office door by which we were enclosed.
"No!" I cried out loudly on a harsh, instinctive sob,
but heedless he approached the door
     and turned the wooden knob
and suddenly the office was engulfed by searing flames;
racing fiery fingers along the building's frame!

And screams of fear and terror echoed through the air
as panic seized the hearts of those, by fire, now ensnared.
"The windows!" I yelled hoarsely. *"To the windows, everyone!"*
And thirty people safely fled; the flames to overcome.
Thirty people touched the ground, but thirty wouldn't do
for on our office staff, there numbered thirty-two! . . .
"Oh, God!" a woman loudly cried as smoke our vision blurred,
"two men are still left in there . . . it's Alex and Peter!"

Quickly, without thinking, I turned and swiftly ran
toward the fiery building where flames, one wall, now spanned.
And climbing through a window,
      my eyes now scanned the room,
searching, ever desperately, across the fiery tomb. . . .
And then I clearly saw them, lying on the floor,
Peter near the cabinets and Alex by a door.
And crawling o'er the wooden floor, heedless of the flames,
I quickly reached the spot where Alex, now unconscious, laid.
Then wrapping my arms 'round him, I dragged him by my side
as singed from scorching heat . . . in pain . . . my body agonized!
Beads of perspiration dripped from off my skin
while smoky, acrid billows, my burning vision dimmed.
But then at last, I saw it, and my hand reached out to touch
the window, as two other men, Alex's body clutched!

Then gasping ever desperately for life's most precious air,
I filled my throbing lungs as flames around me brightly flared
and turned, despite the desperate shouts
      from people in the street,
to rescue now my enemy before I made retreat! . . .
Again, I crossed the wooden floor, reaching Peter's side;
praying God would help me . . . deliverance to provide.
And pulling Peter, painfully, across the flaming room,
I prayed that by the fire, our lives wouldn't be consumed!
I prayed that God, in mercy, would deliver us from death

as torturously I labored o'er each and every breath. . . .
And then once more the window, my hand did firmly grasp,
as near complete exhaustion, o'er fresh air I gasped!

◇◇◇◇◇◇◇

Two weeks went by and then our staff assembled once again;
within another building the Company did rent.
And work resumed its normal pace, to a hectic rushed degree
as people soon forgot about the fiery catastrophe. . . .
Oh, how quick disasters fade from people's minds;
how quickly they forget about the difficult, trying times!
How quickly they resume, again, patterns of routine,
forgetting e'er the times when God, in mercy, intervened!
And so I once more found myself ignored and clearly snubbed
by those within the office, my friendship e'er rebuffed.
And though the vicious rumors and hateful dirty jokes
seemed to have dissipated with the fire's smoke,
I found myself, nonetheless, treated with disgust
by those who look on Christians with antagonism.
And Peter viewed me ever with hatred and contempt;
seeking, by his cold rebuffs, my hurt and detriment.
And so my heart, with bitter pain, cried out to the Lord,
"Is this the bounty that I reap for kindness e'er outpoured?"

But then I thought of Jesus, dying for mankind;
dying for the very ones His holy Name maligned. . . .
I thought of Him e'er whispering as spikes his body slew,
"Father, please forgive them, for they know not what they do."
And somehow, thoughts of Jesus softened all my hurt,
for I had suffered nothing of the pain that He endured!

◇◇◇◇◇◇◇

But then, one day, a boy named Lou; a quiet office clerk,
approached me as I left the office building after work.
"You know," he said, *"I've watched you*

> o'er these past few years;
> the way that you respond as people laugh and mock and jeer.
> I saw the way you risked your life, others thus to save,
> and sense you really care for them, despite how they behave.
> And somehow, I just know there's something deep inside of you
> that's truly well worth having, despite how misconstrued."

And so with deep-felt reverence, I led him to the Lord.
And now on earth, for Christ, there stands another ambassador!
Now there stands a mighty voice speaking out for God,
as Lou, into His Kingdom, many souls e'er draws!

And o'er these fleeting past few years, he's turned into a man
whose vibrant life and faith in God, respect and awe command.
And some of those who mocked at me,
    who laughed and loudly jeered
have come . . . through Lou . . . the Savior's Name
    to honor and revere!
Oh no, not hateful Peter; the Gospel he still scorns
as being just for weaklings, those feeble-minded, born.
But then, perhaps, someday he'll come, the Savior to embrace;
I don't think he is, after all, a truly hopeless case,
for how could I have ever guessed that Lou would come to be
a valiant man of God and fellow-heir, eternally? . . .
And how could I have known I'd play so big a part
in touching, through Lou's ministry, so many needy hearts?

But then I think of Jesus, his triumph o'er the grave;
and all the Hell-bound captives his mercy ever saves. . . .
I think of all the souls, that by his blood will ever stand
upon the Shores of Heaven as countless grains of sand.
I think of all God's children; sparkling as the stars
who form one tiny diamond in his hands . . .
    by nail prints scarred.
And somehow, thoughts of Jesus humble all my pride,
for I am just one tiny flame reflecting forth his Light!

MAN OF OBEDIENCE

Color me purple, orange and tender green;
glimpse my heart, love's devotion seen.

"Who then is the faithful and sensible slave whom his master put in charge of his household to give them their food at the proper time? Blessed is that slave whom his master finds so doing when he comes. Truly I say to you, that he will put him in charge of all his possessions."

Matthew 24: 45–47

"... blessed ... are those who hear the Word of God and obey and practice it!"

Luke 11: 28b (Amplified)

*H*e was a simple, humble man, righteous before God
not for deeds of greatness, noble actions done,
but for a heart that listened, intently, for God's Call;
ready to obey Him, despite what might befall.

And so . . .
He took a journey down a narrow, lonely path;
a journey overshadowed by a sacrificial task.
A journey that would bring him suffering and pain,
and even call to question the goodness of his name.
But loving God, he understood that virtue doesn't rest
on man's applauds, earth's acclaim—his humbleness to test.
He understood that approval comes from God on High, alone
who ever tests the hearts of men, their spirit fully known.
And loving God, he understood the price he had to pay
to tenderly protect the lives within his hands, God laid.
Loving God, he understood, entrusted to his care
was a woman and her Child; God's holy Name to bear.

Joseph . . .
heard the angel's voice, in his dream to speak,
"Take Mary as your wife, on earth, and raise her Godly Seed.
Raise the One within her womb as if your very own,
yet know He is man's Savior, sent from Heaven's Throne!"
And Joseph never faltered, but took Mary as his wife,
despite the scorn of others; mean and hurtful lies.
For how could people comprehend, with hearts so cold and hard
the purity of two young lives, and God's omnipotent part? . . .
"Illegitimate child," their Son would e'er be called;
their name linked with disgrace, judged of moral fault!

Joseph . . .
heard the angel's voice, in his dream to speak,
"Take the Child and his mother; into Egypt flee!

*And stay there until I call you back, once more, into this land
for evil seeks to kill this Child and end God's holy Plan."*
And Joseph never faltered, but took his wife and Child
into a vast and desert land; a foreigner to dwell.
Far from friends and kindred, far from all he knew,
he labored, ever faithfully, providing home and food.
Ever caring for the needs of these very special ones;
safety and protection, the goals he never shunned.
And never did he stop to ask, "What's in this for me?"
God's will, alone, was his reward; no glory did he seek! . . .
Strangers did surround him in this Land of Bondage, past
but trusting in his God, alone, he carried on his task.

Joseph . . .
heard the angel's voice, in his dream to speak,
*"Take the Child and his mother, Egypt now to leave.
Return again to Israel, the land from which you fled
for those who sought the young Child's life,
	truly, now are dead."*
And Joseph never faltered, but rose from that night's sleep
and traveled with his family, Israel's land to reach.
And hearing God's Voice speak to him, warning in a dream,
he journeyed on to Galilee; Nazareth to seek.
For through God's holy prophets, Scripture did foretell
that Nazareth would be the town
	in which this Child would dwell.

And so . . .
he settled in that land, a carpenter by trade;
a craftsman whose mighty hands, useful objects made;
fashioning each piece of wood into a unique form,
other lives to benefit; their dwellings to adorn. . . .
And he, too, like a piece of wood, was fashioned by God's hands;
other lives to benefit; fulfilling God's own Plan.

Joseph . . .
he was a simple, humble man, righteous before God;
no words recorded that he spoke, no mighty actions done.
And yet deeds of obedience, faith and love expressed,
commitment to his God outpoured—all mankind to bless!

"And this is love, that we walk according to His commandments."

II John 6a

"And Joseph . . . did as the angel of the Lord commanded him . . ."

Matthew 1:24

PORTRAIT OF HYPROCRISY

*Color me blue, green and yellow;
glimpse my heart, deceptive and shallow.*

"Not everyone who says to Me, 'Lord, Lord,' will enter the kingdom of heaven; but he who does the will of My Father who is in heaven. Many will say to Me on that day, 'Lord, Lord, did we not prophesy in Your name, and in Your name cast out demons, and in Your name perform many miracles?' And then I will declare to them, 'I never knew you; Depart from Me, you who practice lawlessness.'"

Matthew 7: 21–23

Yesterday I painted a portrait in my mind
of a man I'd thought about for quite some length of time.
His form I brushed with grayish hues; a dim and misty blur,
shadowed e'er with ashen tints . . . duplicity contoured.
For from his heart, stained black by selfishness and pride,
there ever flowed deception in its dark, pretentious guise.
And while he chose to follow God with mighty actions done,
his heart remained devoid of love, spurning God's dear Son.
Yet following Christ's footsteps, he left his home and friends
to journey e'er in search of Heaven's royal diadem.
And side by side with zealous men,
       he shared forth God's great truths;
words of hope and comfort for the lonely and abused.
And everywhere God led him; he touched men's needy souls
with miracles of wonder . . . God's mercy e'er bestowed.
For God had truly granted him mighty, awesome gifts;
the power, in God's holy Name, Satan's strength to sift.
And men and women, everywhere, in awe did testify
of how this man of miracles brought healing to their lives;
curing them of sickness, healing their disease,
as from the grasp of Satan, their captive lives were freed.
And yet this man, forever, was imprisoned in his soul;
a captive of the greediness his nature did enfold;
a prisoner, forever, enchained within a cell,
converting, on his earthly death, into the pit of Hell.

And so I brushed around him searing, vibrant flames;
a scorching wall of fire consuming all his gains.
For all his mighty actions, his gifts and miracles
did burn within the depths of Hell . . . ashes e'er to cull.
And all his deeds of sacrifice, forsaking home and friends
as kindling wood did merit naught but a fiery, cinereous end!

And then my mind brushed o'er his face
        a mask of tarnished bronze;
brownish hues of putridness, with human skin to bond,
a mask of cruel deception; pretense fused with hate,
compassion, with a charming smile, to e'er dissimulate!
For though his smile bespoke concern for people e'er distressed,
t'was naught but just a cruel facade, inert and lifeless;
the means of gaining for himself the favor he did seek,
the confidence of zealous men, their trust to e'er deceive.
And though he smiled agreement
        o'er the truths of God he heard,
his heart did e'er respond to Satan's subtle, tempting words!

Again, I brushed the canvas deep within my mind
with color to reflect this man, his spirit to outline.
And thus, I stroked perverted lips with tints of icy blue,
for all his noble words of care, his heart did e'er eschew.
And though he spoke of selflessness, of giving to the poor,
his heart begrudged an offering, unto his Lord outpoured! . . .
Oh, n'er was found within his soul warmth and sympathy;
naught but chilling pride and greed within his heart did beat.
And while his words reflected forth the Standards of our God,
his care o'er all the needy was a spiritless facade.
For tasting of God's power, drinking of his might,
he chose, instead, to satisfy his greedy appetite! . . .
And thus, his soul was traded for his own financial gains;
bartered o'er enchantments of Satan's masquerade.

And so, at last, my mind did paint the portrait's final touch;
coins of gleaming silver, his greedy hands to clutch.
And silver coins I painted, in place of human eyes,
for thirty pieces equaled his soul's destructive price. . . .

Thirty pieces was the worth invested on the Man
who spanned the universe as God . . . salvation to extend!

Thirty coins of silver were deemed of greater worth
than the One discipling him, his "Master" upon earth. . . .
But thirty pieces only bought Hell's furnace, with a kiss.
Yes, my friend, this portrait's of a man e'er named Judas!

PRAYER WARRIOR

*Color me orange, purple and yellow bright;
glimpse my heart, in Heaven's light.*

"... and the twenty-four elders fell down before the Lamb, having each one a harp, and golden bowls full of incense, which are the prayers of the saints."
Revelation 5: 8b

"May my prayer be counted as incense before Thee; the lifting up of my hands as the evening offering."
Psalm 141: 2

"... put my tears in Thy bottle; are they not in Thy book?"
Psalm 56: 8b

She stood before the Presence of the Great and Mighty King,
joining with the multitude, his praises now to sing
as dressed in regal garments, whiter than earth's snow,
she left behind all suffering and pain and heartache known.
HEAVEN!—shining brighter, forever, than earth's day;
her Savior's glorious radiance, forevermore displayed
was now her soul's abiding; magnificence undreamed,
the realm of endless splendors throughout eternity!

But as she saw the brilliance of Heaven all around,
she sensed within her being, unworthiness profound.
For earthly gifts and talents were meager in her life;
nothing, of much value, had she to sacrifice. . . .
And no gift of the Spirit that mighty men did claim
could she present now to her Lord in honor of his Name.
Her crown was plain and simple, unlike all the rest,
"nothing," she thought sadly, *"my precious Lord to bless."*

But as she reached to clasp her crown, to lay before his feet,
she heard to her amazement, his voice, her name repeat!
"My child," He whispered softly, *"I am so glad
                    that you are here.
I have waited for this Special Day through many earthly years.
And now at last, you are with Me, where time can n'er erase
the ever sweet communion we will share here, face to face."*

Reaching forth his arm, she now saw within his grasp
a vial of purest gold, his fingers tightly clasped.
"These are all the precious tears," his voice now gently said,
*"that you have shed for loved ones; in intercession, pled . . .
Many nights while others, in comfort's dreams, did sleep,
your spirit did commune with Me, and for great burdens weep.
I knew that I would find you, when the battle grew intense
upon your knees, in earnest prayer, others to defend.*

*I knew that I could count on you to share the heavy load
of burdens others carried, in heartache all alone . . .
In lonely, darkened hours when I scanned earth for a friend,
I would hear you call My Name; faithful to the end.
And all the wondrous fragrance of your passioned, caring soul
did fill the Courts of Heaven, for all there to behold.
For with great faith you understood neglected words of truth,
that where two share a burden, my Spirit ever moves
to crush demonic strongholds, releasing captive hearts
that I might grant the blessings I am longing to impart."
"Oh, do not think,"* He gently said,
        *"great deeds you've never done,
for with your sacrificial prayers,
        great victories have been won!"*

Then suddenly in answer to his clear, unspoken call
a young girl stepped before Him, radiant and whole.
"You prayed for me," she softly said,
        *"when no one on earth cared;
you fought the battle for my soul, and never did despair. . . .
You knew He would deliver me from Satan's evil schemes
and covered me with faithful prayers; my life to ever plead."*

"I, too, am one for whom you prayed," came another voice.
And looking now, beyond the girl, she recognized a boy;
one who wandered down sin's path; rebellious through his life,
scorning righteous counsel, ever prone to strife. . . .
"You prayed for me," he gently said, *"despite my wicked ways,
prayed that God, in mercy, would save me from Hell's flames.
Yet until this very moment, you never knew I'd be
part of this great multitude, Heaven's joys to reap.
For only with my dying breath did I call upon the Name
of the One who died for me, upon the Cross was slain.
And only when I stood before his awesome Presence here,*

did I know you'd prayed for me
        through those rebellious years."

Then joining with the girl and boy, other saints stepped out;
strugglers all, upon earth's sod whom her prayers had touched.
One by one, they spoke of how the burdens in their lives
had been, on earth, made lighter by
        the tears in prayer, she cried . . .
And every tear was gathered in that vial of purest gold;
nothing lost, but cherished; the compassions of her soul.
Every prayer she whispered through the silence of earth's night
was valued far above earth's gold, in Heaven's holy light.

"Do you see, My precious child," the King now softly said,
"these saints are all your jewels; your crown's anointed gems!"
And as she slowly lifted, now, the crown from off her head,
she saw a dazzling brilliance, through Heaven's Courts reflect!
For covering her golden crown were many glowing jewels;
glistening bright, with faces, of those who by her stood. . . .
And bowing now . . . in wonder . . . no earthly joys compared,
she laid before the Mighty King her dazzling crown of prayer!

"You will also be a crown of beauty in the hand of the LORD, and a royal diadem in the hand of your God."

Isaiah 62: 3

" . . . my brethren, dearly beloved and longed for, my joy and my crown . . ."

Philippians 4:1 (KJV)

REVERSAL

Color me yellow, green and blue;
glimpse my heart, pride's attitude.

"Then the Lord said, 'Because this people draw near with their words and honor Me with their lip service, but they remove their hearts far from Me, and their reverence for Me consists of traditions learned by rote, therefore behold, I will once again deal marvelously with this people . . . and the wisdom of their wise men shall perish, and the discernment of their discerning men shall be concealed.'"

Isaiah 29:13–14

"Good evening," said the Pastor,
    his warm smile flashing bright,
"I welcome each and everyone to our fellowship tonight
and trust that you may sense God's loving
    Presence in our midst,
for He cares for everyone, his love is infinite! . . .
And now I offer each of you the opportunity
to share with us your prayer requests,
    your blessings, and your needs;
to share how God has guided you or just your favorite verse."
"Now my friends," he lightly said, "who's going to be first?"
A woman quickly raised her hand and rose from off her chair,
"I will, Pastor," she exclaimed, "a verse, I'd like to share."
Then turning to the Book of Psalms, these words she did impart,
"'Delight thyself in the Lord; He will grant
    the desires of thine heart.'"
"Oh, Pastor," she said happily, "God is e'er so good,
for yesterday, He granted me a dream since my childhood!
Yesterday, a lawyer called o'er my uncle's death
and told me of his thoughtfulness; his generous bequest,
for Uncle Henry willed to me the wooden antique clock
that o'er two hundred years ago,
    my great-grandfather bought! . . .
Oh, how I've dreamed of owning it since days of early youth,
but always thought, upon his death, it'd pass to cousin Ruth.
But now the Lord has given me this very special gift,
oh, isn't God e'er good to us, our spirits to uplift! . . .
And truly, t'was a miracle, for ever prone to sin,
Uncle Henry e'er remained a vile and lost heathen.
And as his sin and wickedness, I never could condone,
t'was over thirty years ago, he last was in my home!"

O'er the church people smiled; God's goodness to commend,
and voices rang out, clearly, with zealous, firm *"Amens."*

Next arose a tall young man, his face wreathed with a smile,
"Praise the Lord," he lightly said, *"to God, we're reconciled!"*
And 'round the church believers, firmly shook their heads,
"Amen," their voices chimed, once more, for Satan they had fled!
"I'd like to have you pray for us," the young man now intoned,
*"for Saturday a group of us will journey to Skid Row
where, should the Lord be willing, we'll reach those needy men
by handing out a paper tract; God's love to e'er extend!"*
Happily he waved the yellow paper in his hand,
*"I'd like to thank, right here and now,
     our zealous brother, Stan.
For all this week he's labored o'er the very trying job
of printing up this paper for the glory of our God.
And t'was his clear, inspired thought
     to print this one-page sheet
in yellow colors, bright and bold, to stand out on the street.
For last year's very poor response, we're sure t'was due, in part
to the paper's dull format, no interest thus to spark."*
"So pray for us," he once more said, *"our efforts, God to bless,
as we seek to stand for Him . . . a bright and bold witness!"*

O'er the church people smiled; devotion to commend,
and voices rang out, clearly, with zealous, firm *"Amens."*

Next, arose a woman with authoritative flair,
pushing back long dark strands of thick and wavy hair.
"I'd like to have you pray with me," she very staunchly said,
*"for three women in our church whom Satan has misled!
Nancy Jones, who seldom comes to worship with us here,
confessed to me desires for a secular career.
Apparently, she's chosen to reject the mission field
and give her heart's allegiance to Satan's tempting deal.
For yesterday she spoke to me of offers she's received
to join with the teaching staff at the University!
And all my ardent efforts to remind her of the Lord*

simply fell upon deaf ears, rejected and ignored.
For scorning special gifts from God, and all my fervent prayers
she simply smiled and said that God could use her . . .
    anywhere!"

The woman paused and shook her head, sighing with regret,
then once more spoke, with deep concern,
    now o'er her friend, Jannette.
"I know that she e'er seeks to glorify the Savior's Name,
but alcoholic beverages, her godliness e'er stains.
For recently invited within her home to dine,
I saw within her cupboard several bottled wines.
And when I spoke of how God's Word condemns Satanic brews,
she spoke of Jesus drinking wine instead of just grape juice!
'Do you really think,' she asked, her voice so very sweet,
'that all the guests drank grape juice
    at the Cana wedding feast?'
'Oh, come, my dear,' she lightly said, her folly to express,
'the sin is e'er in drunkenness; one's drinking to excess.
And if our fellow Christians, for drinking wine are shunned,
then truly, we dishonor God's very own dear Son!'

"Oh," the woman now exclaimed, *"I never was so shocked,*
for all these years, I've thought Jannette a servant of our God!
But now I know the awful truth, she's followed Satan's lures;
seeking worldly pleasures instead of God's Standard.
For how could godly Christians, such sin ever indulge?"
"Oh," she said quite fervently, *"'tis truly pitiful!"*

"And then there's Lori Barten," she very sadly said,
"who's struggling o'er deep problems
    with her second husband, Fred.
And anger and resentment, to me, she has expressed,
but I mustn't say much more . . . t'will break her confidence."
"So please," she said with deep concern, *"pray that God, above*

will free these women from their sins,
  and bless them with his love!"

O'er the church people smiled; compassion to commend,
and voices rang out, clearly, with zealous, firm *"Amens."*

But then arose a quiet man, a stranger in the church
who quoted from the Scriptures, a thought-provoking verse.
" *'God does not delight in pious deeds or sacrifice,*
but a broken, contrite heart, He never will despise.' "
"You know, my friends," he gently said,
  "I've sought to follow God
through all the years that, by his grace,
  I've walked upon earth's sod.
But though I've tried to honor God, my life has not been pure;
for often, I have found myself enticed by Satan's lures.
And often, I have stumbled as I've journeyed down life's way;
crying bitter tears of pain as from God's path, I've strayed.
And for great crimes of wickedness, I truly stand condemned,
for often I have been deceived by Satan's stratagem!
And while I yearn to honor God . . .
  my heart's most fervent wish,
evil sins, in thought and deed, have filled me with anguish."

"Oh," he cried with passion, *"how I long to share God's love;*
to touch some lonely, needy soul with His Spirit from above,
to minister compassion; wounded hearts to bless,
to share with troubled, aching souls, his love and forgiveness.
For while I am a sinner, in naught but pauper's rags;
of purity and virtue, unable e'er to brag,
I know my God still loves me and seeks, my soul to heal;
for mercy and great kindness, to me, He e'er reveals.
And while my deeds of wickedness, His Spirit ever grieves,
his dauntless love, a cord of hope, within my soul still weaves.
For by his deep compassion and costly sacrifice,

*I'll stand before God's holy throne; a pure and spotless life.
And swept e'er from my memory will be my sins, so great;
nor will my eyes e'er cry, again, the tears of deep heartache.
For all my faults and failures; a great and mighty sum,
are washed away, forever, by the blood of God's dear Son!
And while I am unable, of worthiness to boast;
redemption's priceless gift, to me, God's love has e'er bestowed."
"But oh," he said, "how fervently o'er wickedness I've weeped;
for though my spirit's willing, my flesh is e'er so weak.
And while I've sought to touch men's lives
      by deeds of righteousness,
my hands are stained with human blood; evil to express.
For human life I've taken o'er selfish, lustful gains . . .
and for my children's early deaths, I truly am to blame!"*

He paused to wipe away the tears that glistened in his eyes,
"Four young sons," he softly said,
      "God's hand took from my side.
And three died in rebellion; violence prone to reap,
following my footsteps; repeating wicked deeds.
For sins of immorality marred their human souls;
horrendous deeds of evil, their spirits to enfold. . . .
Adultery, lust, and murder touched our home and lives,
but t'was no more than they e'er saw, in me, exemplified."

Clearly now he faltered, unable more to speak
as memories flooded o'er his mind of pain and anguish, deep.
And lives once dear and precious flashed before his eyes;
sons whose forms, within his soul, were vivid and alive. . . .
But then once more, his voice rang out; shaking with concern,
"Oh," he cried, "my Christian friends,
      please heed what I have learned!
Seek with all your heart and soul to love our mighty God,
expressing with devotion, his compassion toward the lost;
remembering all the wretchedness that mars your human soul,

*the fact that, only by his grace, can any life be whole.
And may your hearts e'er overflow with true humility,
for only by his wondrous love, is any soul redeemed!
Only by his graciousness will any of us stand
reflecting forth his purity in Heaven's timeless land."*

Quietly, the stranger once more resumed his chair
as sixty zealous Christians, in icy silence, stared!

"Well, my friends," the Pastor said, now rising to his feet,
"it's time we bow in prayer and close
      our meeting for this week."
And people 'round the church, now quickly bowed their heads
as polished words of eloquence, the Pastor clearly said . . .
*"Dear and loving Father, we thank You for Your care
o'er these godly, zealous saints . . . Your Name to proudly bear.
We thank You for enabling us to stand before the lost
as servants, in humility, bearing forth Your cross.
And most of all, we thank You for the joy and deep-felt peace
in serving You, unshackled, from Satan's wicked schemes! . . .
And now we truly praise You for granting Mary Lou
the antique clock she'd dreamed about
      since early days of youth.
And thank You for her faithfulness, all evil to despise;
her life of humbled godliness, n'er to compromise. . . .
For those who seek to honor You, in righteousness e'er steeped,
will find that, in return, great blessings they will reap!"*

*"And so we claim Your blessings and guidance to bestow
upon this group of fine young men
      who will journey to Skid Row
in hopes of sharing forth Your love with lost and godless men
whose lives have suffered ruin by the folly of their sins.
Oh, may You honor each young man for giving of his time
to share forth Your compassion with*

> *these poor, impoverished lives. . . .*
> *And thank You for the insight that You've given Brother Stan*
> *in printing up this yellow tract, according to your Plan!"*

Clearly, now the Pastor paused upon a heartfelt sigh;
prelude to the sinfulness his lips did e'er decry.
"Oh Lord, our hearts are heavy o'er
      these sisters who have strayed
from following their Savior down life's rocky, narrow way.
And with each one, we pray there'll be conviction of their sins
that o'er deceptive wickedness, victories they might win!
And may each woman turn again, a godly life reclaimed
by shunning Satan's subtle lures; all evil to disdain. . . .
For though we all are human and our flesh is e'er so weak,
victory over evil, in You, is ours to reap.
For Satan is a conquered foe, by Your Hand subdued,
thus evil need not conquer those who, truly, follow You!"

"And so we stand with confidence, Satan to rebuff,
sharing forth, with needy souls, Your holiness and love;
praying for believers whose lives are ever stained
by human faults and weakness, discrediting Your Name.
Praying that You'll grant those weak, unstable souls
the knowledge that their sinfulness cannot e'er be condoned! . . .
For only in relinquishing the pleasures of their sins
can they ever grow in grace, victories thus to win!
And only as they boldly stand, clothed in holiness,
can they e'er reflect Your love, other lives to bless.
For when one seeks the path of sin, dishonoring Your Name,
naught but shame and sin's disgrace o'er his soul can reign.
And when, in pride, one mocks Your Laws
      and shuns Your strict commands,
'tis folly to believe he'll find reward on Heaven's Land!
So bless these saints who follow You in true humility,
serving You with godly lives and holy, righteous deeds.

*Bless these saints who ever stand, sharing forth Your love;
reflecting, by their righteous lives,
      Your Son who reigns above! . . .
And now we ask Your blessing on our sister, Ann Magee,
for providing our refreshments of coffee, cakes and tea."*

O'er the church people smiled; their Pastor to commend,
and voices rang out, clearly, with zealous, firm *"Amens."*

◇◇◇◇◇◇◇

The man stood by the entrance to the bright and spacious hall,
gazing now, in silence, as people laughed and talked,
sharing with their Christian friends words they sought to hear;
gossip fused with piety behind a kind veneer.
And voices rang with laughter; happiness expressed,
as people spoke of how the Lord,
      their lives had richly blessed! . . .
But suddenly a silence filtered o'er the room
as people saw the stranger, a welcome to presume!
And timid souls glanced, cautiously; suspicion spawning fear,
while stronger souls glared, angrily, their countenance severe . . .
And in one corner of the room, sipping cups of tea,
the Pastor and two Elders watched him, warily;
praying for God's wisdom in dealing with this man
whose life of sin and wickedness did mock Salvation's Plan.
For n'er would true believers commit such horrid sins
were they Christ's disciples . . . their salvation genuine!
N'er would all God's holiness, so tragically, be scorned
by any saint who, by Christ's blood, truly was reborn. . . .
And n'er could God's own trusting flock ever be allowed
to mingle with a heretic, the Counterfeiter's child! . . .
And so the Pastor swiftly strode across the wooden floor,
"Friend," he said, *"best walk with me, now,
      to the church front door."*

◇◇◇◇◇◇◇

A crisp cool breeze embraced the man, walking down the street;
drying by its gentle touch, the tears upon his cheeks.
But never could its gentleness and ever soft caress
heal the wounds that marred his soul from cruel intolerance. . . .
"*It would be best for everyone,*" Pastor Smith had said,
"*if you would journey elsewhere, for we've not been misled.
We've seen you as the Devil's tool, reflecting forth his creed
by the life of sinfulness that, tragically, you lead.
For godly saints, the Bible says, continue not in sin,
but o'er the Devil's stratagem, decisive victories, win!
So my friend, I think it wise you journey on your way . . .
and may the God of Mercy, your wicked soul still save!*"

Tears, once more, did glisten in the stranger's bright blue eyes;
reflecting forth the anguish with which his spirit cried! . . .
Oh, how he hoped they would understand
      the meaning of Christ's love;
how he prayed enlightenment to touch them from above!
How he longed to stand with them before God's holy Throne,
singing praise, with one accord, for all God's mercy shown. . . .
And how he longed to greet each one as beloved fellow heirs;
reigning in God's holy Realm; eternity to share!

But now his hopes all faded 'neath their cruel, unkind regard;
human souls he n'er could touch . . . so very cold and hard.
Human souls who saw him as a dreaded, hated foe;
accomplice of Satan to lead them down Death's road! . . .
Failing e'er to understand that Satan's stratagem
    numbed their hearts, by righteous pride,
        to all their faults and sins.
Failing e'er to understand that Satan stood e'er clothed
in pride o'er human righteousness; God's grace to overthrow.
Failing e'er to understand that all men were the same;
captives bound, apart from grace, to Satan's dark domain.
And none, of moral excellence, before God's Throne could brag

for pride taints human goodness as vile and filthy rages! . . .

"Oh Lord," the stranger cried now in the depths of his own heart,
"forgive these ones, who by their pride, Your holiness e'er mock.
Forgive them for the arrogance with which
         they scorn Your Son;
for haughtiness of spirit . . . humbled souls to shun.
Forgive them for their folly in heeding Satan's lures,
believing, by their efforts, Your favor is procured. . . .
And help them, Lord, to understand; their blinded eyes to see
that Jesus bowed to wash the dirt from off the traitor's feet;
kneeling as a Servant before the very one
who turned on Him, in hatred, for a meager, paltry sum.
Oh, grant these souls Your wisdom; Your truth to comprehend
lest judgment e'er await them upon their journey's end!"

Slowly now the stranger raised his tear-filled eyes,
silently, to gaze at countless stars up in the sky;
to marvel o'er the universe God's hands, in love, had made;
to sense God's Hand of Favor, upon his spirit laid;
knowing he had honored God by standing on earth's sod,
sharing with the Church, on earth, God's great compelling Law;
that only by God's wondrous love and costly sacrifice
can any soul upon the earth e'er gain eternal life. . . .
And knowing that God's message, he faithfully proclaimed
to Christians 'round the earth whom Satan's ploys o'ercame,
he lifted up his manly voice, praising God with Psalms,
that by his hand, were written o'er many centuries, gone.

And suddenly this stranger vanished off earth's sphere;
forevermore to stand before the God his soul revered.
Forevermore to walk the golden streets of Heaven's Realm;
to wear, before God's angels, a dazzling royal crown.
Forevermore to raise his voice; songs of praise to sing
to the God who honored him as David . . . Israel's King!
And David said . . .

"... to Thee, O Lord, I lift up my soul. For Thou, Lord, art good and ready to forgive, and abundant in lovingkindness to all who call upon Thee ... I will give thanks to Thee, O Lord my God, with all my heart, and will glorify Thy name forever. For Thy lovingkindness toward me is great, and Thou hast delivered my soul from the depths of Sheol."

Psalm 86: 4b-5, 10b, 12–13

"I have proclaimed glad tidings of righteousness in the great congregation. . . . I will not restrain my lips. . . . I have not hidden Thy righteousness within my heart; I have spoken of Thy faithfulness and Thy salvation. . . . Thy lovingkindness and Thy truth will continually preserve me. . . . Let those who love Thy salvation say continually, 'The LORD be magnified!'"

Psalm 40: 9–10, 11b, 16b

SACRIFICE OF LOVE

*Color me blue, red and orange;
glimpse my heart, broken and torn.*

> "*Save me, O God, for the waters have come up to my soul. I have sunk in deep mire, and there is no foothold; I have come into deep waters, and a flood overflows me. I am weary with my crying; my throat is parched; my eyes fail while I wait for my God . . . I am afflicted and in pain . . . O God, hasten to deliver me; O LORD, hasten to my help!*"
>
> **Psalm 69:1–3, 29; 70:1**

I clutched the little icy hand, as bitterly I cried,
for Tommy, my own precious son, in my arms had died. . . .
In agony, great tears of pain my body now outpoured;
pleading, ever desperately, his life to be restored.
But all in vain I agonized o'er each labored breath;
praying God, in mercy, to deliver him from death.
And all in vain I held him, kissing his dear face;
for n'er could I, despite my wish, his ebbing life replace. . . .
And now he lay so very still, cold within my arms;
his happy laugh and sparkling eyes, no more my soul to charm.
No more would that sweet, loving voice gently call my name;
whispering, *"I love you,"* my heart to e'er enchain.
No more would those small boyish arms hold me, oh so tight,
as gently into bed, I tucked him lovingly each night.
And never more would I behold my dear and precious son,
o'er bright fields of flowers, gaily laugh and jump and run.
"Oh dear God," my aching heart in agony now cried,
"Why did You take Tommy? . . . why? . . . why? . . . why?"
"Oh God, You could have saved him, for all things You control,
and by Your hand of mercy, are many miracles!
To You, all things are possible, however great or small;
surely death, o'er one small boy, Your hand
    could have forestalled.
Surely You, in mercy, forever just and good
could have let my Tommy grow into manhood . . .
Surely, from death's awesome grasp and terror o'er the grave,

the child You placed within my womb could have,
    by You, been saved!"
"Oh God," I cried out bitterly, *"I just don't understand;*
where is all Your loving grace, mercy and compassion?"

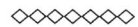

◇◇◇◇◇◇◇

"It was by faith that Abraham offered Isaac as a sacrifice when God was testing him. Abraham, who had received God's promises, was ready to sacrifice his only son, Isaac, though God had promised him, ' Isaac is the son through whom your descendants will be counted.'"
Hebrews 11:17–18 (NLT)

A card came in the mail, today, from a loving friend;
o'er my Tommy's death, condolences she sent.
And at the bottom of her card, with heart-felt sympathy,
she wrote of tears she, too, had cried o'er Tommy's passing.
"I know," she said, *"there are no words*
    to still your aching heart,
but, oh my dear, God is there; his solace to impart."
And then she penned two verses, found within Hebrews
that spoke of sacrifice and a humbled attitude . . .
Had it come from someone else, my soul it would offend
for verses of that sort, my bitterness augments.
But coming from my dear friend, Anne,
    the message gripped my soul,
for as a cripple, all her life, she'd tasted suffering, full.

And so I took my Bible and settled down to read
of Abraham and Isaac, and an awesome destiny . . .
Asked, by God, to sacrifice his dear and precious son,
Abraham arose; all arguments to shun.
And walking toward the mountain where the sacrifice would be,
all God's words of promise, his spirit did concede.
All those precious memories of that special, promised lad

were sacrificed, within the heart, of this biblical nomad.
And all his deepest longings; his tender, cherished dreams,
were offered up, within his heart, for the God he did esteem . . .
Oh, the thoughts of agony that flooded o'er his mind
as he took his precious son; his hands and feet to bind!
Oh, the pain that godly man, so long ago, did feel
as, before God's wishes, his spirit humbly kneeled.
Oh, the faith and deep felt love, toward God, he did command
to raise o'er his son, Isaac, a sacrificing hand!

And then I sensed within the troubled depths of my own soul
what I knew, my dear friend Anne, had prayed I would behold;
the reason God had tested his servant, in this way
was for love and faithfulness e'er to be displayed.
And love is only valid if it's unconditional;
if from a heart without demands, it freely overflows.
For love has little meaning if it's given to the Lord
only in return for all his blessings, e'er outpoured.
And love for God must rest on Who He is, not what He does
or else 'tis just a mockery, and truly valueless! . . .
So glimpsing love's devotion that burned within his soul,
I came to know love's meaning through Abraham of old.
And yet, for me, God's purpose I could not understand;
for Isaac, God restored to his servant, Abraham.

◇◇◇◇◇◇◇

"This is real love. It is not that we loved God, but that He loved us and sent His Son as a Sacrifice to take away our sins."

I John 4:10 (NLT)

Silence whispered to me; a stillness o'er the room
that spoke to me of Tommy, within an earthly tomb.
His laughing voice now echoed, clearly, 'cross my soul;
giggling bursts of happiness that o'er my spirit rolled . . .
But to my human, listening ears, his voice I could not hear,
and so once more, my eyes o'erflowed with bitter, painful tears.
"Oh God," my soul in agony, once more, loudly cried,
"Why did You take Tommy? . . . why? . . . why? . . . why?"

And then somewhere within the bleeding
      depths of my own heart,
I clearly heard God speak to me; his solace to impart.
"Oh, My dear and precious child," He whispered soft and clear,
"why are you so very slow, My Essence to revere?
Where is all your loyal faith, your trust, and hope in Me?
Where is the devotion you professed so ardently?
Was all your soul's allegiance worth no more than your son;
his earthly death, by My hand, e'er to overcome?
And is your love dependent on what I've done for you;
a Contract of Conditions, within your heart to rule?
Am I worth no more to you, than blessings e'er outpoured,
from the wealth and splendor, in Heaven's Kingdom, stored?"
"Oh, My child," He gently said, *"you need to learn the price*
of love that spanned the universe, for your eternal life!

"Do you know," He softly asked, *"what you're worth to Me;*
the value that's been placed upon your soul, eternally?
Do you know how much I paid; your soul's redeeming price
by sending forth My only Son, as your sacrifice? . . .
And do you know the mighty truth, that only through his death
could your soul be ransomed, and your life be fully blessed?"

"Oh, n'er could you conceive of all the pain that I endured
when My Son left My side and journeyed down to earth.
N'er could you conceive of all the agony I felt

as My Son was tortured to save your soul from Hell.
And n'er could you conceive of all I suffered on that day,
when My Son, upon that cross, your ransom fully paid . . .
Oh, n'er forget, My precious child, that I have suffered loss
as My Son lay dying upon that wooden cross.
And for your life, and for your love, I traded My own Son,
seeking, by His painful death, your priceless soul, e'er won! . . .
"I watched from Heaven's sidelines with pain and agony
as spikes were driven, fiercely, into his hands and feet.
Every drop of precious blood, his dying form did spill,
was sacrificed according to the dictates of my will;
sacrificed so that, of Heaven's splendors, you might share;
you . . . My precious child . . . a priceless, valued heir!
And every thorn that cut into his pure and sinless brow,
My will, with deep-felt agony, fully did allow.
For else sin's awesome, costly debt never could be paid,
and you, My child, from Satan's grasp never could be saved."

"But tell Me, now, My dictates; all My just demands,
list all the conditions of salvation's costly plan . . .
Tell Me the requirements, upon you, I have placed;
the merits of your worthiness, apart from saving grace.
Tell Me of your deeds of love, upon Me, e'er bestowed
that place Me as your debtor; life's blessings toward you owed.
And tell Me of the goodness that dwells within your heart,
that makes you ever worthy; salvation to impart . . .
And then upon my precious Son, may you fully gaze;
seeing all the painful scars his body e'er displays.
And as your eyes behold nail prints
    within My Son's own hands,
may love's deepest meaning your spirit understand.
And may your spirit ever grasp the pure and holy truth
that as I love My precious Son . . . so also, I love you."

◇◇◇◇◇◇◇

> "Then Jesus said to His disciples, 'If any one wishes to come after Me, let him deny himself, and take up his cross, and follow Me.'"
>
> **Matthew 16: 24**

The crucifixion story I, once more, slowly read
and thought of Jesus' sacrifice; his dying in my stead.
I read of how He gave his life, willingly, for me
that with Him, I might live and reign, throughout eternity . . .
And as I read the story, I came to understand
the meaning of His Sacrifice; the love it did command.
For through the cross, God's matchless love, I clearly did behold
and saw the value that He placed upon my sin-scarred soul.
And through the cross I came to see the deep, compelling love
that Jesus had in living by his Father's will, above . . .
"Not My will, but Thine be done," He earnestly had prayed,
and then He sacrificed his life, so that I might be saved.

And now I heard his gentle voice, calling o'er my soul;
asking me to lift my eyes, his nail prints to behold;
asking me to touch his wounds, those deep and wretched scars,
with which his body, glorified, ever will be marred . . .
And in my heart, his gentle voice seemed to clearly say,
"This is what love looks like, child; the way love is displayed.
And how could you e'er know My love except you come to see
the sacrifice I freely made that day on Calvary?
How could My compassion, you ever understand
had I not come to earth, a Sacrificial Lamb? . . .
How could you e'er comprehend the depth of My own love
if not for these nail prints and scars I bear, above?"
"And how could you reflect My love, others to redeem,
if there's no cross of pain for you; love's mark of suffering?
For love, My child, is sacrifice . . . the giving from your soul
of all, from Me, your human heart seeks to e'er withhold . . .
And n'er forget that, willingly, I left My throne above,

to stand upon the earth I made, devoid of all but love . . .
So lift your cross, My precious child, and follow after Me
that others, through your pain-scarred life,
  God's love may clearly see!

◇◇◇◇◇◇

" . . . I bear on my body the [brand] marks of the Lord Jesus [the wounds, scars . . . these testify to His ownership of me.]!"
Galations 6:17b (Amplified)

Humbly, now before God's throne, my broken spirit bowed;
freed, at last, from all demands, so arrogant and proud.
For now I saw most clearly, through God's own spotless Lamb,
that all my heart's devotion had just been a talisman;
service rendered to my God; a sacred, magic charm
that in return, would offer me protection from all harm;
the means of e'er protecting me from suffering and pain,
assurance that God's mighty hand,
  all hurt would e'er restrain . . .

But God had never saved me to live just for myself;
to make of Him, my servant . . . all suffering to dispel!
T'was I who was the servant, called to do His will;
called to empty forth myself that He, my life might fill . . .
And I, too, was my Father's child, asked to suffer loss
that love's devotion to my God might triumph o'er my cross;
that other lives might come to see, reflected through my pain,
sacrificial marks of love, to glorify His Name . . .

And so as love flamed, deeply, within my pain-scarred soul,
my hands released to God the boy they e'er did tightly hold . . .
"Oh God," I prayed upon the altar, deep within my heart,
"Tommy, I now give to You; all rights to e'er discard.
And may You take this sacrifice . . .

poured out with tortured pain,
and use it e'er to glorify Your precious, holy Name!"

◇◇◇◇◇◇◇

"... The LORD called Me from the womb; from the body of My mother, He named Me ... In the shadow of His hand He has concealed Me, and He has also made Me a select arrow; He has hidden Me in His quiver ... surely the justice due to Me is with the LORD, and My reward with My God."

Isaiah 49:1–2, 4b

A deep, abiding sense of peace flooded o'er my soul
as slowly to my feet, I now once more arose.
For in my heart, I knew that God, *"Who doeth all things well,"*
was holding Tommy in his arms; all suffering e'er dispelled! ...
I knew that God had called him forth to stand before His Throne
that all of Heaven's splendors, to him, might now be known.

And then across my mind, there flashed a vision of his face,
wreathed with joy and happiness, all earthly pain erased ...
And on the canvas of my mind, I clearly saw my son,
o'er Heaven's dazzling splendors gaily laugh ...
    and jump ... and run!
And then I saw my precious Lord bow on Heaven's land,
and scoop my son, e'er lovingly, into his nail print hands;
holding him e'er closely with more love and tenderness
than any finite human, ever, could express!

And in my heart, I cried with deep devotion to my God,
for Tommy, by those nail prints, stood on Heaven's sod!
And in my heart, I thanked God for his nail-scarred Son above,
who died upon a wooden cross ... a Sacrifice of Love.

SOWING IN VAIN

*Color me orange, blue and tender green;
glimpse my heart, in striving deceived.*

"Do not be deceived, God is not mocked; for whatever a man sows, this he will also reap."

Galatians 6: 7

*H*appily, the little boy reached into the bag
his chubby hand probing deep, a tiny seed to grab.
Then bursting with excitement, he raced across the yard
and dropped his seed into a hole; a healthy plant to start!
Quickly, chubby little hands pushed dirt over the seed,
patting down the soil, in haste, excitedly. . . .
Then racing fast into his house; jumping up and down,
he proudly told his mother of his seed within the ground!

Every day the little boy ran out from his back door
over to that mound of dirt in which the seed was stored.
And with all of the diligence a little boy could claim,
he labored o'er that spot of dirt, a lovely plant to gain! . . .
Daily, from an empty can, fresh water he outpoured
on the thirsty, sun-baked ground; moisture to restore.
And as the weeds rose from the soil, he pulled them one by one,
confident that, soon, he'd see a thriving plant begun!

But days went by—and then the weeks—and no plant ever grew
despite the water he outpoured; the weeds he did uproot. . . .
"You must work even harder," his mother firmly said.
"Don't give up; just spend more time in tending it, instead."
And so the boy worked harder than he ever had before,
watering and hoeing and fertilizing more. . . .
But all his zealous efforts, sadly, proved in vain
for just a barren mound of dirt that little spot remained!

And then, one day, as angry tears streaked his sunburned face,
the little boy dug up the hole and found his big mistake. . . .
And suddenly he realized what he couldn't understand;
suddenly he knew just why he couldn't grow that plant.
For lying there within the soil was what his hands had sown,
not a tiny, healthy seed, but just a lifeless stone!

SWORD OF PEACE

*Color me red, tender green and orange;
glimpse my heart, passionate and poignant.*

"Woe to those who call evil good and good evil; who substitute darkness for light and light for darkness; who substitute bitter for sweet and sweet for bitter! Woe to those who are wise in their own eyes, and clever in their own sight!"

Isaiah 5: 20–21

The man stood on the sidelines and watched the brutal fight
as one boy slugged the other with a left and then a right,
and blood poured out of nostrils, streaking swollen lips,
as one head now collided with the granite of a fist
and blackened eyes shut, painfully, against another blow
as blood, like tiny raindrops, splashed across the snow. . . .

"Help!" the small boy whimpered as he fell upon his knees.
"Help me!" he cried hoarsely, *"help me, someone, please!"*
But then I saw the stranger . . . the tall and silent man
walk up to the bully and pat him on the hand! . . .
"Enough," he said in quiet tones; a gentle manly voice.
"Let's go," he said, his arm around the boy to hold him close.
And side by side they journeyed down a wide and snowy path,
talking in low undertones, reproofs e'er wed with laughs! . . .

"No!" I cried out angrily, in shock and disbelief
that one could be so callous, those cries for help not heed!
"No!" I shouted tearfully, gazing on the form
of that small and frightened boy . . . alone, his torment borne.
"No!" I cried in wonder that a man could be so cruel
to let a small boy suffer . . . the bully to approve!
But then as if in answer to my angry, pulsing cries,
I saw that man pause and turn, with pity in his eyes.
And suddenly sheer terror gripped my aching soul
for on that quiet stranger, *my* face, I did behold!

◇◇◇◇◇◇

> *"But if any of you lacks wisdom, let him ask of God, Who gives to all men generously and without reproach, and it will be given to him."*
>
> **James 1: 5**

Darkness vanished swiftly; the curtain of the night,
as running from that frightening dream, I opened up my eyes
and felt warm rays of sunshine gently brush my cheeks
assuring me that, from such dreams, I e'er could make retreat!
But in my mind persisted the vision of that man,
my own face etched upon him; indifference thus to span! . . .
And somehow, deep inside me, I knew that awesome dream
spoke to me of something that I needed to perceive.
But what? . . . I pondered thoughtfully,
 laboring through the day;
what was it that awesome dream was seeking to convey?
I had never seen a child abused, so very cruel,
nor championed a bully who ignored the Golden Rule.
Nor had I e'er refused to help a lonely soul in need;
to lend a helping, outstretched hand; man's suffering to relieve.
So why? . . . Why was I now haunted by this specter of myself;
this man whose very character, my own soul did repel?
And how was I to understand what all of this might mean?
"Oh Lord," I prayed with weary sigh, *"help me, somehow, see!"*

◇◇◇◇◇◇◇

> "For if you . . . intermarry with them . . . know with certainty that . . . they shall be a snare and a trap to you, and a whip on your sides and thorns in your eyes, until you perish from off this good land which the LORD your God has given you."
>
> **Joshua 23: 12–13**

Snow was softly falling, reflected in the lights
that hung above the city streets like shimmering gems on high.
And laughter crackled loudly across the cool, crisp air
as children raced from store to store, their secret thrills to share.

But driving home that evening, the flurries on my mind
were fears and doubts and problems I had battled for some time.
And far from all the beauty of nature's velvet rug,
the problems that I battled formed a dirty, icy slush. . . .

Julie . . . such a pretty girl I'd married at nineteen,
but oh, what pain and heartache
     through this marriage I had reaped
as o'er the years I struggled to love her as a wife
but found, for all my effort, only tension, pain and strife! . . .
Oh, how could I have known, at such an early age
that pretty on the outside . . . and the inside . . .
     weren't the same?
How could I have understood; a carefree, happy youth,
that lies are often packaged as counterfeits of truth?
And how could I have known that what I thought was love
would prove to be a lashing whip . . . it's force, my soul to cut?

No . . . t'was but mockery of all that God had planned
when He fashioned woman and brought her unto man.
And what was termed a marriage, by solemn toned decree
was nothing but an ugly and warped facsimile! . . .
And yet how could I hurt her, after all these years?

How could I withstand the force of bitter, angry tears?
And then there were the children . . . precious, every one;
my sweet and lovely daughter and happy, boisterous sons;
treasures that I value far above earth's gold,
diamonds that e'er sparkle in the depths of my own soul!
And how could I deprive them of the one who gave them birth,
who, by her very presence, must instill a sense of worth? . . .
"No," I muttered thoughtfully, sensing deep despair,
"I've got to make a go of it . . . for everyone's welfare."

◇◇◇◇◇◇◇

"Do not think that I came to bring peace on the earth; I did not come to bring peace, but a sword . . . And a man's enemies will be the members of his household."

Matthew 10: 34, 36

"Vindicate the weak . . . Do justice to the afflicted and destitute. Rescue the weak and needy; deliver them out of the hand of the wicked."

Psalms 82: 3–4

I heard the angry shouting before I reached the door,
Julie on the warpath . . . a scene that I abhorred!
And glancing through the window, I saw my forceful wife
walking toward my youngest son, cowering with fright. . . .
"You will now obey me!" she yelled in violent tones
as Jason whimpered softly; a low and frightened moan.
"Y . . . y . . . yes . . . ma'am," he stuttered nervously,
    backing off with dread
as Julie's form loomed nearer; a monster o'er his head! . . .

And then with all the swiftness of a lunging bird of prey,
she grabbed his arm and shook him; anger to display.

And suddenly she slapped him . . . hard across the face,
as blood ran from his nostrils, his upper lip to trace!
"Listen when I talk to you!" she bellowed in his ear,
"Y . . . y . . . yes," he stuttered once again, shaking now with fear.
And then I saw the teardrops glisten in his eyes,
and knew that I must intervene to save his threatened pride.

"Julie," I said gently, as I walked into the room;
seeking in a quiet way, to stem the pending doom,
"enough of all this yelling," and then I reached a hand
to gently touch her shoulder, attention to command
as Jason cried out hoarsely, *"Help me, Daddy, please!"*
And suddenly . . . with horror . . . I saw my hellish dream!

◇◇◇◇◇◇

"I will cry unto God Most High, to God who accomplishes all things for me. He will send from Heaven and save me . . . God will send forth His lovingkindness and His truth."

Psalm 57: 2–3

"The Lord supports the afflicted; He brings down the wicked to the ground."

Psalms 147: 6

Sleeplessly, I tossed upon my lonely bed that night,
darkness hiding all the tears of bitter pain I cried
as o'er my mind now focused my dear son's precious face,
streaked with tears, contorted . . . by angry blows, misplaced;
blows that left a sightly mark for people to behold;
blows that left him bleeding, corrupting his own soul;
blows that would, fore'er remain, wretched memories
without the balm of healing grace . . . and love's tender mercy!
"Oh God," I cried in anguish, *"show me what to do.*

*I've always sought to be a man whose life would honor You.
And You have e'er commanded us to turn the other cheek,
to look upon our enemies with love, and not retreat.
And You bore all the violent hate, the bitter lashing blows
that mankind heaped upon You, in cruelty, bestowed.
And truly, You have told us to bear, each one, his cross;
to sacrifice all selfish dreams; all earthly values, lost. . . .
So what am I to do, dear Lord? . . . Tell me, Jesus, please!"*
I prayed, as near exhausted, I drifted off to sleep.

◇◇◇◇◇◇◇

Then suddenly I found myself looking up with awe
into the face of One I knew must be the Son of God!
"Follow Me," He gently said, and led me by the hand
out into a wilderness . . . across the burning sand.
And side by side we journeyed on, just the Lord and me,
into a small old village where the people sought healing.

"Jesus . . . Master, save us!" came the anguished cries
of men and women writhing in pain too great to hide.
And suddenly from out their midst, came a wretched boy,
foaming and convulsing; the Devil's captive toy.
"Help him, Lord!" I pleaded, shocked by all his pain,
but Jesus stood and looked at me, then gently spoke my name.
*"How can I deliver him? . . . Wouldn't it be cruel
to vanquish off the Devil, and free him from his rule?
Better that he suffer, until in pain he dies,
then that My hand should free him; Satan to defy!"*

"No, my Lord!" I answered, stunned with disbelief,
"You are all victorious; all evil You defeat!"
"Well said, My son," He answered, *"truth you have discerned,
for God's love e'er demands that evil be o'erturned."*
And then while people stared at Him,
      in wonderment and doubt,

Jesus turned and touched the boy, *"Be healed,"*
               He said outloud!

Once again, we journeyed across the desert plains
until we came to stand within a city of great fame;
a city bright as amber, burnished in the sun,
a city that I recognized as Jerusalem! . . .
And Jesus led me safely down ancient, cobbled streets,
walking with a purpose that guided now, our feet
until, at last, I saw it . . . the Temple on the hill
and felt my Master beckon me, my walking thus to still. . . .
Quietly, we stood there and listened to the sounds
of profiteers and hawkers within the Temple grounds,
shouting in loud voices, selling forth their wares;
turning God's own earthly House into a thoroughfare!

"Lord," I cried in anger, *"stop this wickedness!"*
But Jesus only looked at me, a firm set to his lips.
"Why?" He asked me suddenly, *"what difference does it make
if people shout, irreverently, within these holy gates?
Why should I be troubled if men defile God's House?
Why should I not tolerate their wicked deeds poured out?"*
"But Lord," I answered quickly,"You are holy, pure, and true;
You can never compromise with the evils that they do!"
"You are right," He gently answered. "God's Spirit cannot stand
side by side with wickedness; Satan's curse on man."
"And don't forget, My precious son," He said in gentle tones,
"you follow Me in holiness . . . My nature for your own."
Then picking up the supple whip his hands had swiftly made,
He strode into the Temple; a Presence none could sway. . . .
And tables crashed upon the floor and coins flew in the air
as hawkers fled into the street in terror and despair!

Once more Jesus led me down dazzling city streets,
but this time, they were paved with gold, a crystallizing sheen!

And walls around the City, instead of bricks and stones,
were made of precious jewels, whose brilliance ever glowed!
And naught but love's pure holiness reflected everywhere;
no pain or tears or suffering for any man to bear! . . .
Oh, the untold splendors of Heaven's glorious Realm;
radiance and beauty; man's soul to overwhelm!

But suddenly before me, a large gate opened wide
and outside, in the darkness, a multitude e'er cried
of men and women destined to spend eternity
within a fiery cauldron; Hell's searing flames to breathe!
"Let us in, Lord Jesus!" their voices loudly wailed,
as tears of bitter agony streaked their faces, pale. . . .
And desperate men and women pleaded, on good works,
a place before God's Presence; salvation's gift deferred!

"Oh Lord," I cried in anguish, sensing their great pain,
"give them just another chance to reverence Your Name!"
But Jesus turned and looked at me; compassion in his eyes,
"No, My son," He gently said, "love n'er can compromise."
"And what you really ask of Me is purity, defiled;
to bend My holy Standard, accepting what is vile. . . .
But love that blends with evil can never be of God
for holiness and purity, that mingled bond e'er mocks!
And how could Heaven be a place of joy for ransomed souls
if evil stood within these gates, and walked the streets of gold?
But n'er forget, My precious son, that I am purely love
and gave My life so all the lost might reign with Me, above.
But I can never compromise . . . with evil thus to dwell,
and so those who reject Me, I banish now to Hell."

◇◇◇◇◇◇◇

> "*Do not be bound together with unbelievers; for what partnership have righteousness and lawlessness, or what fellowship has light with darkness? . . . 'Come out from their midst and be separate,' says the Lord, 'and do not touch what is unclean; and I will welcome you. And I will be a Father to you, and you shall be sons and daughters to Me . . .'*"

II Corinthians 6: 14, 17–18

> "*Ah, sword of the LORD . . . How can it be quiet, when the LORD has given it an order?*"

Jeremiah 47: 6–7

Darkness swirled around me as I opened up my eyes,
and suddenly I knew it was the middle of the night. . . .
And I was lying in my bed, far from awesome dreams,
back into reality . . . or so that's how it seemed.
But somewhere, deep inside me, I knew beyond all doubt
that reality had altered by the vision God allowed.
And in my heart, I sensed ahead decisions to be made
and knew, at last, I'd have the strength, God's leading to obey!
For being just like Jesus, I too must stand apart;
free from bonds of evil, my living soul to mar. . . .
And I must fight for righteousness, and free the captive ones;
those whom God has given me, my daughter and two sons.
For by his strength and power, Jesus set me free
to live a life, abundant, with joy and victory! . . .
And how can I deny Him when He freely gave his all?
How can I deny his love; his holy, righteous call?
How can I e'er mingle with what belongs to sin
and yet expect God's favor and blessings, thus to win?
For following my Master means walking in his steps;
reflecting forth His Nature . . . without any regrets!

And now, at last, I understand love's high exacting price,
for 'tis God's will, in holiness, all sin to sacrifice. . . .
Now, at last, I understand what Jesus asks of me;
to know his will and do it . . . in his strength . . . fearlessly!
And now, at last, I understand just why He sent a sword,
and how, for peace, it cuts across each sinful, binding cord! . . .

"I love You, my Lord Jesus," I cried into the night,
"and I will stand before You, and fight for what is right!"
And in my heart as, wearily, I drifted off to sleep,
I heard my Savior's gentle voice,
    "Well done, My son . . . I'm pleased."

THE ACCIDENT

*Color me blue, red and orange;
glimpse my heart, in suffering transformed.*

" . . . *with humility of mind let each of you regard one another as more important than himself; do not merely look out for your own personal interests, but also for the interests of others."*

Philippians 2: 3–4

"Bear one another's burdens, and thus fulfill the law of Christ."

Galatians 6: 2

The man walked slowly down the street that Sunday afternoon
and passed a gang of boys who laughed
      and called him, *"The Baboon."*
And looking on I understood just why that name they chose
for he had a large flat head and grotesque cheeks and nose.
And even in his awkward walk and badly twisted shape,
he clearly did resemble a large and ugly ape!
And seeing just the humor that the situation held,
I found myself unable, my unkind thoughts to quell. . . .
So shedding forth the somberness
      with which my face was masked,
I joined with that gang of boys
                and laughed
                        and laughed
                              and laughed.

The man walked slowly down the street
      that early Wednesday morn
and passed a gang of boys who loudly
      mocked and jeered and scorned
and mimicked all his gestures in a bold and obscene way
while throwing at his crippled form rocks of hardened clay.
And seeing just the humor that the situation held,
I found myself unable, my unkind thoughts to quell. . . .
So shedding forth the somberness
      with which my face was masked,
I joined with that gang of boys
                and laughed
                        and laughed
                              and laughed.

The man walked slowly down the street late that Friday night
and passed a gang of rowdy boys looking for a fight.
"Hey . . . Baboon!" they fiercely yelled as in his face they spit.
"It's time our might and power you fully did admit!"

So twisting his arm, roughly, they forced him to his knees
and yanked his hair and slapped his face
      despite his earnest pleas.
And someone forced an ape-like mask o'er his swollen face
while on his flat and ugly head a black straw hat was placed.
Then laughter crackled in the air while drunken boys did whirl
in a mocking ape-like dance, their anger to unfurl.
And seeing just the humor that the situation held,
I found myself unable, my unkind thoughts to quell. . . .
So shedding forth the somberness
      with which my face was masked,
I joined with that gang of boys
                and laughed
                        and laughed
                              and laughed.

◇◇◇◇◇◇◇

I never saw the car that day as I crossed the street,
but only heard the horrible and terrifying screech.
And when five long weeks later, I opened up my eyes
I saw a sight so frightening that I wished that I had died! . . .
My face, all smashed and purple, was an ugly swollen mass
and my body, maimed and crippled, was resting in a cast
while tubes were stretched from everywhere
      to life-support machines
making me resemble some Frankensteinish fiend!

Oh the pain and suffering, for months, that I endured
as I laid upon that bed of agony, secured.
And ceaselessly my mind did spin with fears and anguish deep,
preventing me from finding any lasting sense of peace. . . .
But when at last, the day arrived that I journeyed home,
I found, within my troubled soul, a seed of hope had grown;
hope that other people, my needs would understand
and out of love and kindness would treat me like a man;
hope that others recognized the all important fact

that each man is of value, no matter what he lacks! . . .
But soon I came to realize the sad and lonely truth,
that all men tend to worship gods
  of wealth, good-looks, and youth.

⋄⋄⋄⋄⋄⋄⋄

I walked slowly down the street that Sunday afternoon
and passed a gang of boys who laughed and called me,
  "The Big Goon."
And fully did I understand just why that name they chose
for I had a large bruised head and swollen cheeks and nose.
And in my awkward clumsiness and badly twisted form,
I knew I had become a man fit for mocking scorn!
And sensing all the anguish that the situation held,
I found myself unable, my painful thoughts to quell. . . .
So turning from that gang of boys, I wiped tears from my eyes,
as in my heart, with sorrow deep,
      I cried
        and cried
          and cried.

I walked slowly down the street that early Wednesday morn
and passed a gang of boys who loudly mocked
  and jeered and scorned
and mimicked all my gestures in a bold and obscene way
while throwing at my crippled form rocks of hardened clay.
And sensing all the anguish that the situation held,
I found myself unable, my painful thoughts to quell. . . .
So turning from that gang of boys, I wiped tears from my eyes,
as in my heart, with sorrow deep,
      I cried
        and cried
          and cried.

I walked slowly down the street late that Friday night
And passed a gang of rowdy boys looking for a fight.

"Hey . . . Big Goon!" *they fiercely yelled as in my face they spit.*
"It's time our might and power you fully did admit!"
So twisting my arm, roughly, they forced me to my knees
and yanked my hair and slapped my face
        despite my earnest pleas. . . .
And fervently I prayed that God would send some help my way;
saving me from these thugs, so wicked and depraved!

Then as my bloodied body slumped upon the ground,
to my ears arose a siren's loud and wailing sound.
And suddenly policemen were running down the street;
footsteps pounding loudly on the cold and hard concrete. . . .
And o'er my battered body there loomed the twisted form
of the man who's suffering I, once, had mocked and scorned.
Tears were glistening brightly in his soft and large blue eyes
as that gang of hoodlums he angrily decried.
And gently did he wipe the blood from off my beaten brow,
while beneath my throbbing head, he placed a folded towel.
"I'm here," he said, *"to help you in any way I can,*
for your pain and suffering, I fully understand!
I, too, was once an object of their cruel and bitter hate,
and at their hands I, too, endured a very similar fate. . . .
So rest assured I understand the pain that you must bear,
for in your hurt and anguish I, too, have fully shared!"

Then silently I listened as he cursed the vicious brawl,
and thanked a kind policeman for answering his call. . . .
And knowing all the mercy that his actions toward me held,
I found myself unable, my grateful thoughts to quell. . . .
So turning toward his twisted form my hand I did extend
as I murmured . . . tearfully,
                  "My friend
                          my friend
                                  my friend."

THE DOLL

*Color me tender green, orange and bright yellow;
glimpse my heart, o'er loneliness struggle.*

"If you then, being evil, know how to give good gifts to your children, how much more shall your Father who is in Heaven give what is good to those who ask Him!"

Matthew 7: 11

Darla O'Neill

"Gentle, dazzling little doll
you are mine . . . after all!
Oh may I always hold you near,
and love you more each passing year."

Tenderly, I lifted my doll from off the bed,
straightening its jacket; stroking soft its head,
as in my mind I whispered the old familiar rhyme;
a tribute I had written to this doll when I was nine. . . .
And suddenly sweet memories arose within my heart;
memories that this special doll was destined to impart.

◇◇◇◇◇◇◇

Oh, how it seems like yesterday I first beheld its form;
large brown eyes . . . thick dark hair . . . clothes so nicely worn,
velvet pants and jacket . . . a pale blue silky shirt . . .
and shoes of softest leather, intriguing a small girl!
"Oh, Mommy!" I cried breathlessly, all of four years old.
"Dolly . . . me want dolly!" as on her arm, I pulled.
"Mommy . . . dolly!" I squealed in childish awe,
         jumping up and down;
pointing at the vision in the tempting toy store, found!

But gently, Mother led me out the large front door,
"No, my dear," she softly said, *"it's not for a child of four."*
And so with angry, heaving sobs, I cried all the way home,
"mean . . . Mommy . . . mean!" I said in quivering undertones.
And when my Mother handed me my little rag doll friend,
I ripped a button, angrily, and left a tear to mend.

But while my childish anger soon spent itself in tears,
that doll remained a longing throughout the coming years. . . .
And then one Christmas morning, I opened up a gift,
and found, to my amazement, the special doll I'd missed!

And looking up with wonder, I found my gracious Mom
smiling at me, tenderly . . . joy flashing through her calm!
"For you, with love, my darling," her gentle voice did say,
"I'm sorry that there had to be such a long delay!"
And in that quiet moment, I came to understand
that love withheld my doll from small, destructive hands!

◇◇◇◇◇◇

And now my eyes glance, lovingly, across the glowing room
and come to rest, with deep felt joy, upon my handsome groom;
the man for God's creating me, to share his earthly life;
to hold me e'er within his heart as lover, friend, and wife. . . .
Oh, many years have gone since I first beheld his face
and hoped, with childish longing, his future to embrace.
And many nights of loneliness had to be endured
while I grew from selfish child to woman . . . strong, mature.
Many nights, in darkness, were spent in prayer to God;
crying . . . in my loneliness . . . bitter, angry sobs.
"You don't care about me," my broken heart accused,
"mean . . . God . . . mean!" I said, *"to hurt me, oh so cruel!"*
Yet all the time, God looked on me in tenderness and love;
holding safe, within his hands, the precious gift I'd crush! . . .

And now as my eyes glance upon God's very special man,
his will . . . in love's withholding . . . I fully understand.
And in my heart, I thank God for his gracious, tender care
for I am so unworthy, his blessings thus to share!
And in my heart, with wonder, I hear God gently say,
"For you, My child, with love . . . despite the long delay!"

THE PUPPET

*Color me blue, orange and red;
glimpse my heart, it's anger spent.*

"To what then shall I compare the men of this generation, and what are they like? They are like children who sit in the market place and call to one another; and they say, 'We played the flute for you, and you did not dance; we sang a dirge, and you did not weep.'"

Luke 7: 31–32

My puppet looked so lovely as she whirled about the floor
that my lonely aching spirit began to rise and soar.
And laughter swiftly vanquished all the gloom from off my face
as Mindy made a curtsy with perfect poise and grace! . . .
Then suddenly she twirled around and danced a lively jig
while auburn curls bounced to and fro upon her stylish wig.
And yellow lace and ribbons gaily swished the cool, still air
as small black shoes clacked, merrily, upon the wooden stairs.

Together now we danced around each corner of my room
and Mindy never faltered as I sang a happy tune
and swung her till my head began, dizzily, to spin;
my fingers cramped with tension from pulling on her strings.
But all at once, I heard a 'pop' and looked about to see
a string from off my puppet's arm, now hanging loose and free!
And while a silly mocking smile still played about her lips,
her left arm dangled, helplessly, about her thighs and hips.

Anger flared within me that this doll could treat me so,
after all the loving care that on her I bestowed! . . .
And so I roughly grabbed her and threw her on the floor,
then turned with indignation, and slammed the bedroom door!

Days went by and still I burned with anger, deep within,
o'er the loss of power that was tied up with that string.
But gradually I came to feel a deep sense of regret
for Mindy had still other strings that were of value, yet. . . .
So grinning rather sheepishly, I picked her up again,
"Mindy," I said kindly, *"let's you and me be friends!*
It doesn't matter anymore about that useless arm;
you still have many other strings
      with which to prove your charm."

And so, once more, we whirled about the corners of my room,
dancing as I sang aloud a now familiar tune.
And Mindy still smiled up at me, forgiveness on her face
as slowly and together, the dance steps we retraced.
'Round and 'round the room we whirled in perfect harmony
and no one could be lovelier than Mindy was to me! . . .
But all at once I heard, again, the echo of a 'pop'
as from her leg, another string did rip apart and drop.
And now she faltered, awkwardly, unable to go on
and silence filled the room where we had danced to happy song.
Then anger burned, again, within the chambers of my heart
and tension gripped my fingers as I tore her cords apart! . . .

"You stupid doll!" I fiercely yelled as ribbons did unfurl
and auburn curls, through the air, my hands did roughly hurl.
"*You're just a worthless puppet . . . of no value,*" I exclaimed,
"*for how can you e'er dance, again, with crippled feet so lame?*"
Then swiftly tossing all the scraps into a bundled heap,
I threw her broken body into the window-seat;
slamming down the wooden lid with bitter, violent force,
cursing o'er my anger's infuriating source! . . .
"*Goodbye to you, dear Mindy,*" I said with biting scorn,
"*o'er such a useless puppet, I'll never grieve or mourn.
For you are not the kind of doll to fill my life with cheer;
your strings are weak and flimsy, unable to adhere. . . .
And I will never waste my time with such a doll as you
who can no longer dance aright to simple, happy tunes!*"

◇◇◇◇◇◇

Months went by and Mindy never crossed my mind again,
for I had found a charming and very special friend!
This girl was, oh so pretty, so very sweet and kind,
that with her I now spent a large portion of my time. . . .
Marcie liked to laugh and sing and dance to happy tunes
and so she quickly vanquished all my loneliness and gloom!

Together, we now spent our days in merriment and fun,
laughing from the early morn till setting of the sun.
And never did I doubt the love and friendship that we shared,
for Marcie, I knew in my heart, about me truly cared!

But then, one day, all laughter was erased from off her face,
as lines of hurt and anger, her features clearly traced.
For sickness claimed my active form and laid me on my bed,
and thoughts of dance and merriment, swift with pain, had fled.
Marcie, I felt certain, would fully understand
and offer me her sympathy with kindly outstretched hands. . . .
But now she stood before me . . . a lioness enraged,
cursing me for spoiling all her happy, carefree days!
Her voice rang loud with anger as she strode about my room
and o'er my bed of sickness, her fearless form did loom.
"How could you be so very cruel?" she asked in angry tones.
"How could you take away from me,
*   the pleasures that I've known?*
Oh, you are not the kind of friend who's loyal and sincere;
no longer do you fill my life with happiness and cheer. . . .
And I will never waste my time with such a friend as you,
who can no longer dance aright to simple, happy tunes!"

Angrily, she glared at me; contempt upon her face.
And then she slammed my bedroom door,
             her footsteps to retrace!
And silence filled my empty house; its presence to impart
a bitter sense of loneliness to dwell within my heart.

◇◇◇◇◇◇◇

With pain I thought of Marcie and the joy she once had been;
of laughing eyes and happy smiles and songs she liked to sing . . .
And suddenly there came to mind another friend, once dear,
whose memory stung my burning eyes
             with wet and glistening tears.

Slowly and most painfully, I crawled from out my bed,
seeking now my little friend whose hair was auburn red.
But lifting up the window-seat, in sorrow I now groaned,
for Mindy lay all mangled on the spot
        where she'd been thrown. . . .
Her hair was coarse and matted; tangled from abuse
and yellow lace and ribbons lay shredded 'round her shoes.
And o'er her battered body lay a grimy film of dust
while buckles on her dancing shoes
        were turning brown with rust.

But Mindy still smiled up at me; pity on her face
as tenderly, her wretched form, I once more did embrace.
And tightly now I drew her to the hollow of my chest
while matted hair and torn clothes, I gently did caress. . . .
Then trembling in my anguish and deep sense of despair,
my sorrow and contrition, I painfully declared.
"Oh, Mindy," I said brokenly, *"I've been such a blind fool,*
for how could I have ever been so brutal and so cruel?
How could I have thought you my gratifying slave;
deliberately rebelling . . . o'er my will to misbehave?
Oh, how could I abuse you, my little wooden friend,
condemning you to suffer such a horrid, wretched end?"

There was, of course, no answer from this puppet in my arms,
who once had so delighted me with all her lovely charms. . . .
But looking down upon her form, I saw reflected back
all the pain and misery with which *my* soul was racked!
And as my fingers gently touched her broken, battered form,
I sensed the depth of sorrow in which *my* spirit mourned.
For *I* had been a puppet . . . a doll upon a string,
dangled by another for the pleasures I would bring! . . .
And so as nightly shadows o'er my lonely being loomed
and darkness laced her fingers 'round each corner of my room,
I held my Mindy closer in a loving, warm embrace,
and cried, in vain, o'er bitter wounds that time could not erase!

THE TOY STORE

Color me green, yellow and blue;
glimpse my heart, life's pleasures pursued.

> "Brethren, do not be children [immature] in your thinking . . . but in your minds be mature [men]."
>
> **I Corinthians 14: 20 (Amplified)**

*T*wo small hands pushed open the door
and the little boy raced into the bright store;
happy, at last, in this Child's Paradise
where hundreds of toys now dazzled his sight!
Oh, how he dreamed of this wonderful day
when, on his own, with these toys he could play!
But now his small mind, marveling did spin
o'er the awesome question . . . where to begin?
Bright shiny trains, sleek flashy cars,
round bouncy balls, and tall candy jars;
rainbows of color splashing a wall,
row after row of magnificent dolls!
T'was more than a small boy's mind could conceive;
visions of grandeur, hard to believe!
So happily, he shrieked with delighted cries
o'er all the opulence meeting his eyes
and clapped his small hands with happy glee;
the store's most enthusiastic devotee!

Then swiftly he raced to a shiny red car,
tossing aside his stale candy bar.
And standing on tiptoes, all by himself,
he lifted the car from off the wide shelf;
stroking the chassis with wet, sticky hands;
holding it close as he quickly ran
to the back of the store where a wide, empty space
enabled him now the car to race! . . .
Roughly, he shoved it across the wood floor,
clapping his hands in excited furor
as the car spun 'round and flipped on its top,
marred by a scratch before it could stop.
And then, once more, it sped 'cross the room,
on a collision course with doom,
for into a wall it suddenly crashed;

a fender and side now hopelessly smashed!
So sadly, the little boy shook his head,
"Stupid old car!" he angrily said.

◇◇◇◇◇◇

Next, he picked up a baseball bat and gave it a mighty swing,
seeing himself in the batter's box;
      the crowd's applause to win . . .
But suddenly another toy swayed and crashed to the floor
and so hurriedly, another aisle, the little boy now explored!

A row of bright and colorful dolls arose before his sight,
their pretty clothes and happy smiles, his small mind to delight.
And as he stared in wonder at their many varied forms,
he felt the urge to take them down and see them all perform!
So reaching up above him, his little hands now clasped
a wooden soldier, gleaming bright, in navy blue and brass.
And turning 'round the metal key within the soldier's back,
he sent him swiftly marching down a narrow wooden track;
laughing as the soldier tipped and toppled to the floor,
his arms and legs still moving to the drumbeat of the Corps.

Next, he took a baby doll with soft and bouncy curls
and held her roughly by the hair, giving her a whirl,
before he pulled the plastic ring, causing "Baby Sue"
to mutter ever sweetly, *"I love you . . . I love you."*
Tossing such a silly doll quickly from his side,
he gaily ran on down the aisle until, at last, he spied
a doll so very lovely, far more than all the rest,
that heartbeats of sheer pleasure fluttered in his little chest!
And big blue eyes now sparkled with happiness and awe
as he stood a'gazin at the soft and lovely doll;
happy he had found her . . . so perfect and so new;
awe-struck by the vision in feathery pale pink hues!

And then two sticky little hands pulled her off the shelf;
a blow to all her loveliness, tragically now dealt
as dirty fingers stroked her hair and wrinkled her soft dress
and chocolatey lips, a firm wet kiss, on her face impressed. . . .
But suddenly her loveliness paled beneath his eyes
for he found no ring to pull . . . his spirit to delight!
She wasn't like the other dolls that marched
      and laughed and cooed;
his childish whims to satisfy and keep him e'er amused. . . .
And so he placed her on the shelf and shook his curly head,
then flounced away with an angry pout,
      "Stupid old doll," he said.

◇◇◇◇◇◇

Racing off now eagerly down another aisle;
a thoughtless, irresponsible, happy little child,
he grabbed a fist of candy from a tall intriguing jar
then pulled, again, from off a shelf a shiny racing car. . . .
But suddenly a giant o'er his tiny being loomed;
a man whose deep and awesome voice echoed 'round the room!
"Young man," the giant roughly said,
      "*look what you have done!*"
"*All the toys you've damaged . . . there's quite a hefty sum!
I think you'd better come with me,*" his booming voice declared.
"*Somehow, all these broken toys will have to be repaired!*"

But now as panic seized him with a fearful sense of dread,
the little boy turned and ran . . . up the aisle he fled;
racing toward the large front door; seeking his escape
from the awesome, giant man who ruled over the place! . . .
Swiftly, little sticky hands pushed wide the wooden door
as little legs raced, feverishly, from out the dazzling store.
And never once did he look back or pause to take a breath,
knowing such a careless deed would prove a deadly step;
knowing that the awesome man was really mean and cruel,

expecting him, a little boy, to cater to store rules! . . .
And so as down the street he ran, he shook his curly head
o'er the pleasures now denied, *"Stupid old man!"* he said.

◇◇◇◇◇◇

The old man sitting on the bench now looked into my face;
a deep and painful loneliness, his features clearly traced.
And as his storytelling came to a poignant end,
tears arose in his eyes, his hollowed cheeks to wet.
"You know," he softly said at last, in a stilted, trembling voice,
*"I was like that silly and foolish little boy.
And now my life is empty, and I sit here all alone,
with naught but bitter memories of selfish pleasures, sown.
And no one here, upon this earth, truly cares for me,
but then this is the bounty that my selfishness has reaped!"*

Slowly and most awkwardly, he rose from off the bench
with a groan of heartfelt pain and misery, intense.
And looking down into my face he wiped tears from his eyes,
"Oh, young man, don't be like me!" he very firmly cried.
*"Give yourself for others, loving till the end,
and in return, you'll find through life, loyal loving friends. . . .
And may you, through the coming years, remember evermore
that life is not some dazzling and meaningless toy store!"*

◇◇◇◇◇◇

Silently, I watched him till he disappeared from sight,
knowing in my heart that his words were fully right;
knowing that those thoughtful words I never could refute,
for what he spoke, I recognized as honest, genuine truth.
And knowing that his loneliness, no words could e'er erase,
I finally turned and journeyed home, my footsteps to retrace;
thanking God He'd given me a loving wife and son;
thanking Him that o'er my selfish heart were victories, won!

And fervently I prayed that God, in mercy, would e'er bless
this man who'd come into my home, at last, a welcomed guest.
But nothing with this lonely man e'er could be regained,
despite our strong resemblance and the sharing of our name.
For thirty years had come and gone since we last had met;
thirty years in which his life, frivolously, was spent. . . .
And I had grown to manhood from a small and awkward boy;
a stranger to this one who filled my childhood with such joy.
And memories I had cherished, so many years ago
were meaningless beside the void he'd left upon my soul. . . .
For never in those thirty years, since I was a lad,
had I seen this lonely man . . . my irresponsible Dad!

The year is 1895, and this story takes place in a small town on the western frontier . . .

TOUCH OF LOVE

Color me red, blue and purple;
glimpse my heart, in brokenness humbled.

" . . . *I will lead the blind by a way they do not know, in paths they do not know I will guide them. I will make darkness into light before them and rugged places into plains. These are the things I will do, and I will not leave them undone."*

Isaiah 42: 16

"*I* hate her! . . . I hate her!" The words pierced the air
as the girl shook her fists with an angry flair.
"Don't ask me to see her again, Mr. Jones,
for when I was five, I was cruelly disowned
by that hateful woman, without any thought
of the horror and pain, in my heart, that was wrought!"

"Oh, how I remember that day, most clear,
for my mother's voice, I still can hear."
'Carrie,' she said, 'I'm going away;
with Mrs. Simpson, you'll have to stay.'
'I love you, my darling,' she whispered so sweet,
then hugged me and kissed me and made her retreat
while in darkness, with terror, I grasped for my Mom,
and cried with deep anguish e'er she was gone!
Oh, n'er could I doubt why she left me behind,
you see, Mr. Jones . . . at five I was blind.
And with such a flaw, I was sure to shame
the goodness and virtue accorded her name!"

"Don't you know, Mr. Jones, of the widespread belief
that blindness is given as punishment reaped
for sins very wicked in God's holy sight;
evil deeds done in the dead of the night? . . .
And so my dear mother weighed forth the cost
and gave me away, lest her virtue be lost!

Now twenty long years have since gone by
and all but hatred within me has died
for that cruel woman who gave me birth,
then scorned me as having no value or worth!
Oh, that sweet deafness would stop my ears
that her hateful name, I'd no more hear!
Oh, that her memory my soul could erase

and all my heredity e'er be replaced!"
"You ask me to see her; you say that she cares?
Please, Mr. Jones . . . such lies I can't bear!
I hate her! . . . I hate her! . . . and wish she were dead!
There, Mr. Jones, it's finally been said! . . .
So go to my mother; tell her sweet lies
if the hateful truth she cannot abide.
But never again ask me to see
the woman I'll hate through eternity!"

A vibrant silence charged the air;
pulsing currents, everywhere

as Mr. Jones turned to go;
emissary of a foe.

And Carrie shook with silent rage;
tortured in a mental cage

as memories from so long ago
splashed on walls within her soul;

memories she could n'er subdue;
pictures brushed with vivid hues . . .

Sunshine kissing dewy lawns;
diamonds sparkling on emerald fronds.

Bluebirds singing in the trees;
soft pink blossoms, bright green leaves.

A woman's lovely chestnut hair;
pale blue eyes in a face, so fair.

Lace and ribbons on the dress
her mother's slender form caressed.

A gentle voice, *"I love you, dear,"*
a flower placed behind her ear

as they slowly journeyed home;
o'er lush fields of flowers, grown.

home from church that Sunday morn;
home . . . where she felt safe and warm,

secure in all the love and care
her mother's presence gave her there.

Trusting . . . as a little child . . .
her mother's words and gentle smile.

Unable e'er to apprehend
that all her happiness, soon, would end.

Unable, then, to e'er believe
that from her presence, her mom would flee

as light turned slowly toward the gray;
twilight in a smoky haze.

And then the haze turned to night
as blackness, finally, cloaked her sight . . .

But on that day, so long ago,
her eyes shone bright with love, aglow

as swiftly, she had stooped to pick
daisies, in a bouquet, thick.

And placed them in her mother's hand;
hoping she would understand

the feelings she could not express,
but felt . . . so deeply . . . nonetheless.

"They're lovely, dear," her mother said,
and bent to, gently, kiss her head.

*"I'll put them in your favorite vase,
and set them in a special place!"*

And so those flowers . . . simple, sweet,
sat in the hall; their friends to greet.

But that was all before the time
when Carrie started going blind . . .

"Wait!" she shouted suddenly, to halt the closing door,
as swiftly, in her anger, she crossed the wooden floor;
reaching for the table, on which was now displayed
a bunch of lovely daisies, in a beautiful bouquet.

Grabbing at the tender stems, she twisted them apart,
ripping, in her anger, at the memories in her heart
until, at last, the flowers fell . . . shreds about her feet,
and weariness replaced the hate with which her spirit seethed!

"Tell my mother, Mr. Jones," her thin voice now intoned,
"these flowers will be buried in the dirt behind this home!"
And as the tall, distinguished man swiftly took his leave,
she prayed, her mother's spirit, her words would deeply grieve.
"Oh, may you taste of agony!" she whispered fierce and low,
"the agony inflicted, once, upon my very soul!"
And then the bitter heartache; within her spirit dammed,

broke in mighty torrents, her will could not withstand
as o'er the endless blackness her eyes forever saw,
tears of pain and agony, once more, began to fall.

◇◇◇◇◇◇

Birds were singing sweetly, nestled in the trees;
Spring was coming early to the town of Willow Creek.
But Carrie didn't hear the birds or feel the sun's warm rays
as she sat upon the porch, reliving yesterday . . .
And so when Mrs. Simpson walked up to her side,
she startled as a timid doe, suddenly surprised.
Gently, with compassion, Mrs. Simpson held her hand
"Carrie," she said softly, *"I truly understand."*
"But all this hate and bitterness you've bottled up inside
will only, in the final end, your own destruction buy.
Don't let the lovely girl you are come to be destroyed;
a vengeful, hateful woman . . . of love and kindness, void.
Don't let those painful memories from so many years ago,
as ugly, vicious monsters, contort your very soul.
For life means ever growing beyond our hurts and pains,
not letting them warp our lives; slaving us in chains . . .
And if what's right and good in life,to others you would give,
then Carrie, oh my dearest, you must learn how to forgive!"

Soft brown eyes gazed, hopefully, at Carrie's pretty face;
lovingly caressing the lines self-pity traced;
searching for an answer to the thoughts that she had shared,
hoping Carrie understood how very much she cared!
But singing birds and barking dogs were all that answered back
as Carrie sat in silence, her anger still intact.
And so as Mrs. Simpson finally turned to go,
she wondered if she, too, had now become a hated foe . . .
But in that very moment, her hand squeezed warm and tight
as Carrie smiled and softly said, *"I know that you are right."*
"You are so wise and knowing, speaking words of truth;

*God was kind and gracious in bringing me to you! . . .
And someday all these memories that stir my mind with hate
will all but be forgotten; by time, alone, erased."*

*"No, my dear," came the soft and ever wise response,
"those memories, o'er the coming years,
         your soul will ever haunt.
For time can n'er erase those wounds, so bitter and so deep,
and if you trust in time, alone, more bitterness you'll reap.
But Carrie, if you stop and look within your wounded heart,
I think you'll find forgiveness,
         toward your mother, to impart . . .
Go deep within that prison where you dwell within your soul
for there, I think, another face you clearly will behold.
And if you find that other face bruised by ugly scars;
a wretched band of thorns; his bloodied forehead marred,
remember, t'was your bitter hate o'er memories long ago
that pressed that crown of thorns in place
         with fierce and painful blows!"*

Long after Mrs. Simpson left, Carrie sat alone,
confronting, in her prisoned soul,
         God's Presence e'er made known;
expressing all the hurt and pain that brewed within her heart,
praying God, in mercy, forgiveness to impart . . .
For loving God, she truly sought a life that honored Him;
despite her deep-felt anguish, true blessings He had given.
And from a child, she sensed his hand touching, soft, her life;
guiding through her daylight . . . into the darkest night! . . .
And so she prayed for victory o'er the hatred in her soul;
a place, within her spirit, where forgiveness could unfold . . .
Then suddenly her soul was touched by God's own gentle peace,
and Carrie knew that bitter hate,
         through her, no more would seethe!

⋄⋄⋄⋄⋄⋄⋄

Autumn leaves were falling, gold and burnish brown,
blowing o'er the landscape of the thriving frontier town
as Carrie slowly made her way down the narrow street,
going forth with trembling heart, her mom at last to meet . . .
But as the tall, distinguished man walked closely by her side,
and pressed her arm with tenderness;
    a kind and thoughtful guide,
Carrie shook with greater fear than e'er her heart had known,
and seeds of horrifying doubt, within her mind were sown!
Panic seized her trembling soul; gripping it by force
as terror launched her spirit down a dark, nightmarish course!
"Run! . . . Run!" raced the ceaseless words across her mind;
mocking all the blindness, by which she was confined.
For everywhere she turned her head; seeking for escape,
her sightless eyes confronted just a thick, black velvet drape.
No escape awaited her down this, her chosen path,
and no one stood to shelter her in such an awesome task . . .
And yet, somehow, within the very chambers of her soul,
she sensed God's loving Presence;
    the raging storm's brunt, lulled!

"Here we are," said Mr. Jones, stopping her at last;
his words so mild and gentle; such a vivid, sharp contrast
to all the fears assailing her on this momentous day,
but then t'was not his mother . . . and he was n'er the prey!
Arm in arm, they mounted a wooden flight of stairs,
their faces flushed from walking in the crisp, cool autumn air.
And then a door was opened and Carrie stepped within
the home from which, instinctively, her spirit ever cringed.
Swiftly, she was ushered to a large and spacious room
where, left alone in darkness, she waited forth her doom;
convinced that to this woman her eyes would never see,
she was no more than, simply, a curiosity;
convinced that in her throbbing heart, no words could ever still
the lonely, painful memories that pulsed against her will;

convinced that she had, after all, made a big mistake
in coming to this dreadful and terrifying place! . . .
But then she heard the footsteps . . . staccato on the floor,
and suddenly a woman's hand opened wide the door
and footsteps came into the room, standing somewhere close,
but then a horrid silence . . . icy cold, arose!

"Carrie," said the woman's voice, calling her at last;
reality now merging with the memories of the past.
*"Oh, how long I've dreamed of you, praying for this day,
but now that you're before me . . . I don't know what to say!"*
A very thin and nervous laugh echoed through the air;
her mother wasn't finding such words easy to share!
*"I'm . . . I'm glad you liked my flowers,
     I've grown them every year;
an ever sweet reminder of memories, precious . . . dear . . .
And always, when those flowers, my fingers lightly hold,
I think about my little girl . . . e'er living in my soul."*
Carrie's fingers lightly touched her tears and trembling lips;
whatever she expected, it truly wasn't this!

"Oh, how I've longed through all these years,"
     her mother softly said,
*"to once more hold you in my arms; to tuck you into bed,
to kiss away those silly tears you cried each time you fell;
all your fearful, childish dread, gently to dispel.
And how I've longed to watch you grow into a lovely girl;
my loveliest, most precious flower, ever to unfurl . . .
But oh, my darling Carrie, t'was never meant to be
for life had forged upon us another destiny!"*

Her mother's trembling voice now broke upon a painful sob
as o'er her aching spirit, memories deeply throbbed.
And Carrie stood, in silence, fighting for control
o'er the tears of agony that welled up in her soul . . .

But when, at last, her mother turned and gently spoke her name,
shock replaced the anguish whirling through her brain.
And Carrie now stood shaking as chills ran up her spine
o'er the awesome knowledge . . . her mother, too, was blind!

"Carrie," called the gentle voice, *"where are you, my dear?"*
"Oh, mother!" sobbed the lovely girl, *"I'm standing over here!"*
And suddenly the years of pain and anguish were erased
as lovingly, her mother's hands, caressed her sightless face.
"Oh yes!" she whispered softly, *"I knew it would be true;*
you really are as lovely as I've always pictured you! . . .
Oh Carrie . . . oh my darling . . . if your father only lived;
if only there had been someone, time and help to give.
But I could never care for you; a woman blind, alone;
raising you . . . my sightless child . . . into a woman grown!
And so as darkening shadows o'er my hazy vision loomed;
the curse of Scarlet Fever when I bore you in my womb,
I knew the time was coming when I had to say 'good-bye,'
when for your sake . . . in agony . . . a part of me would die . . .
And someone else would hold you, and rock you in their arms,
calming all your fears, protecting you from harm.
And so that day, so long ago, I put you from my side;
praying God, Who e'er sees all, your path would closely guide.
Praying you would grow into a woman, wise and fair,
knowing in the Simpson's home love and tender care . . .
And praying you would n'er forget,
      through all the coming years,
that once, you'd had a mother to whom you were most dear!"

"Oh, Carrie," said the gentle voice, *"I love you, oh so much!*
And now, at last, your precious face,
      my hands can once more touch!
Now, at last, I clearly feel the outline of my dream,
for through my hands and fingers, your beauty I have seen . . .

*And now I know that o'er these years of loneliness and pain,
God was truly guiding you; my prayers were not in vain!"*

"Oh, mother!" Carrie softly cried, kissing her sweet face;
holding her e'er tightly in a loving, warm embrace
as darkness turned to dazzling light deep within her soul;
pictures bright with joy and love no human eyes behold . . .
And all the bitter memories of her lonely, hateful past
vanished in her mother's arms . . . safe, secure, at last!

TRADEMARK OF EVIL

Color me red, green and blue;
glimpse my heart, atrocious and cruel.

"And He said, 'Take heed that you be not misled; for many will come in My name, saying, 'I am He,' and 'the time is at hand'; do not go after them."

Luke 21: 8

"*If* you make me your earthly King,"
 his voice rang loud and clear,
"I promise you I'll rid each town of sin within the year.
Intolerant fanatics will be the first to go
for we will never tolerate the divisiveness they sow!
Then we'll focus next upon those poor and wretched fools
who think that God will tolerate the breaking of his rules!
All those who flaunt our moral laws;
 who lie and cheat and steal,
we'll vanquish e'er their values, in our children, they instill . . .
One by one, we'll rid each town of everyone corrupt
and those who follow righteousness will raise the Victor's Cup!
For God has truly led us; freedom to possess
as wickedness we conquer, dispensing forth justice!"

The crowd cheered loud and joyfully o'er such a forceful speech
and prayed to God that this was now the man they long did seek.
And words of adoration, they raised unto his name
while in their zeal and fervor, they spread abroad his fame. . . .
And when, at last, the day did come to crown a mighty King,
this man did stand before them; the Victor's Song to sing!
And men and women, everywhere, cried joyful tears anew,
for now they had this royal King . . . all evil to subdue!

◇◇◇◇◇◇

True to all he promised, the new King lost no time
in seeking out the people who did practice wicked crimes.
And to each one, he spoke these words
 of judgment, most severe;
warning that resistance would be met with all they feared! . . .
"Repent of all your wicked deeds," he very firmly said,
"conform to what's expected of your family and your friends;
or else, by all the power that, from God, I do possess,
I'll banish you from off this land of peace and righteousness!"

*"Now if God's Name you'll honor and from evil clearly part,
raise to me your forehead and receive this numbered Mark,
for else we cannot know you from the wicked, evil ones
who terrorize this world, through hate and corruption! . . .
Resistance, we will not accept . . . I warn you, think again,
of terrorists who called on God to save them, in the end!
And in God's Name, they did great acts of evil to mankind;
so now all such fanatics . . . like them . . . the sword will find!
For standing here, before you, I represent The Law;
I am God's voice now in this world; protecting one and all.
And for the sake of all mankind, who wish to live in peace;
all who stand opposed to me, great suffering will reap! . . .
So if you wish to save your life; to prosper and survive,
then pledge now your allegiance to my kingdom . . .
  vast, worldwide.
And only with my Mark upon your hand or on your head
will daily food be given for your family to be fed. . . .
For if you wish to buy or sell and prosper in this place,
it must be clear to one and all that the King, you do embrace!"*

So those who did receive the Mark did prosper in each town
where conformity and tolerance did, everywhere, abound. . . .
But those who stern refused the Mark
  were banished in disgrace;
forced to leave their homes and jobs and flee as birds of prey;
viewed as fearful terrorists . . . fanatics with great zeal;
intolerant of harmony within the One World Sphere!

And so the King's good subjects weren't troubled anymore
by wicked, evil people whom they hated and abhorred! . . .
No longer did they need to gaze, with fear and hate's contempt,
upon the ones who did refuse the King's most just request!
No longer did they need to hear the words they long despised
of loyalty to another King; the Savior Jesus Christ. . . .
No longer did they need to share rich bounty from earth's sod

with those who saw them, ever, as unholy and "the lost!"

Now the land was filled with the compliant and the free
who wore the numbered Mark as protective liberty!
And all those, thus identified, as loyal to earth's King
trusted in the goodness his earthly reign would bring;
knowing he would deliver them from evil, evermore;
from the hand of poverty . . . terror . . . and the sword!

And so across earth's boundless lands,
      one mighty name was praised,
for one, alone, from evil, their lives had clearly saved!
One, alone, had overcome the bigotry toward man;
the prejudice that spoke in terms of right and wrong demands!
One, alone, delivered them from binding, rigid force;
allowing each to live his life; a self-determined course. . . .
And so with adoration, their voices loud did ring,
"All praise to our triumphant God . . .
      our King, our King, our King!"

"And he causes all, the small and the great, and the rich and the poor, and the free men and the slaves, to be given a mark on their right hand or on their forehead, and he provides that no one should be able to buy or to sell, except the one who has the mark . . ."

Revelation 13: 16–17

". . . And I saw the souls of those who had been beheaded because of the testimony of Jesus and because of the word of God, and those who had not worshiped the beast or his image, and had not received the mark upon their forehead and upon their hand; and they came to life and reigned with Christ for a thousand years."

Revelation 20: 4

WORDS OF COMFORT

*Color me yellow, blue and green;
glimpse my heart, hyprocisy seen.*

"What use is it, my brethren, if a man says he has faith, but he has no works? Can that faith save him? If a brother or sister is without clothing and in need of daily food, and one of you says to them, 'Go in peace, be warmed and be filled,' and yet you do not give them what is necessary for their body, what use is that? Even so faith, if it has no works, is dead, being by itself. . . . You see that a man is justified by works and not by faith alone. . . . For just as the body without the spirit is dead, so also faith without works is dead."

James 2: 14–17, 24, 26

$\mathcal{T}$he ringing of the doorbell jarred me to my feet,
"*Who,*" I thought with anger, "*is arousing me from sleep?*"
For glancing at the clock that sat beside my bed,
I noted now the time, half-past one, it read.
So hurriedly I grabbed my robe and tied it 'round my waist,
as down the darkened hallway, I stumbled in my haste;
hoping that who e'er it was would have the decency
to note my mild annoyance and very quickly leave! . . .
"*All right,*" I said, "*I'm coming,*" as the doorbell
      chimed once more,
and pulling back the metal lock, I opened wide the door.

There upon the threshold stood a shivering rain-drenched man
who I barely recognized as my good friend, Dan! . . .
"*Hello,*" he said quite hoarsely, as his body shook with cold,
"*I'm sorry to awaken you . . . to be so very bold,
but I'm really in an awful spot, and have nowhere to turn;
no one else around here to show any concern!*"
"*Dan,*" I said quite warmly, "*there's no need to explain. . . .
come on in before you freeze to death out in that rain!*"
Quickly, now I led him into the living room;
the posture of a servant, swiftly to assume
as a glowing fire, I very quickly built,
and made some strong black coffee to chase away the chill.
Then, at last, I settled down in my favorite chair,
ready now to listen to whatever he might share.

His bluish lips were trembling as he very slowly spoke,
revealing that his body, still, was icy cold.
And so I listened carefully, hoping he would see
the interest that I took in him, in this, his Hour of Need!
I couldn't quite hear every word . . . he muttered in a slur,
but eventually, I understood the meaning of his words . . .

Apparently, he took his boat and journeyed out to sea;
the balmy weather tempting him, irresistibly.
But suddenly this storm arose with violent, pounding force,
blowing his small sailboat totally off course!
And barely did he manage to keep his boat upright;
fighting for control as daylight turned to night . . .
But somehow, near exhausted, he made it back to shore;
his car to finally reach through the horrible downpour.
But then, with wretched luck, his old car swiftly died,
leaving him now stranded in the middle of the night! . . .

Then recalling that our home was half a mile away,
he left his car and journeyed here, without any delay;
knowing that about him, I very truly cared;
happy e'er to meet his need, my substance gladly share!
So fondly now I smiled at him . . . my ever trusting friend,
"More coffee?" I asked warmly, as the pot I did extend . . .
And then I sat back, leisurely, in my favorite chair
as words of warmth and comfort, I fully sought to share.

"Believe me," I said kindly, *"I truly understand,"*
and gave his icy form a pat with my outstretched hand.
*"Stormy, violent weather I, too, have fully seen;
no need to educate an old fisherman like me! . . .
Why, I remember just last year, one awful storm-racked day
when I went out fishing along the wind-swept bay.
And as the waves began to toss my flimsy little boat,
my stomach gave an awful heave as, violently, I choked!
And desperately I grabbed the boat's rocking, rolling side,
wondering if the awesome storm, I'd manage to survive! . . .
But mercifully, the storm front, very quickly, lulled
and so my flimsy little boat, into the shore, I rowed."*
"Oh," I said sincerely, *"I fully understand
all that you've experienced in that sailboat, Dan . . . Dan?"*
Drowsily, he gazed at me, clearly half asleep;

and fondly, I smiled back at him with kindness and pity,
for I knew, so very well, exactly how it felt
to battle o'er the elements, their force, my body pelt.
For that storm, a year ago, I rapidly did flee,
left me with a vicious cold to battle for a week!

I looked at Dan and thought now of the mercy God had shown
in allowing that old car of his to break down near my home!
"I'm glad you've come," I gently said,
    with warmth and kindly cheer,
but Dan made no response . . . my words he didn't hear.
"Dan!" I called out loudly, now with deep alarm,
for barely did he rouse as I firmly shook his arm! . . .
And o'er my spinning mind, a fearful thought now mulled,
"Dan," I said at last, *"you should go to the hospital."*
But gazing up into my face, his eyes dismal and bleak,
he muttered now the fateful words, *"I haven't any money."*
"No job," he hoarsely whispered, *"no insurance I can claim;
no doctor's gonna see me if I'm not able to pay."*

"Oh," I sighed now feeling a deep sense of despair,
"I . . . I'd gladly loan you the money,
    but the extra I can't spare!"
"You see," I hastened to explain as he drifted off again,
"my savings . . . for retirement . . . is money I can't spend! . . .
And what I have at the moment, must last the next few weeks;
money for expenditures . . . life's necessities!"
"Oh, Dan," I muttered hoarsely, *"what a truly awful time;
you've caught me, I'm afraid, in a monetary bind!"*
But then a thought crossed my mind; I know t'was of the Lord,
"Dan," I gaily shouted, *"I can, a taxi afford!"*
"You barely live three miles away,
    so the taxi fee, I'll gladly pay."
"And there's no need," I paused to add in a very kindly tone,
"to repay my generosity . . . it's a gift and not a loan!"

Later, as the taxi swiftly drove away,
for my good friend, Dan, I fervently did pray. . . .
"Lord, bless him," I now said in the depths of my own heart,
"and thank You for allowing me to share and have a part!"
Then sensing that Dan's throbbing soul,
      my words and deeds consoled,
I quickly walked into my house, lest *I* catch a cold!

◇◇◇◇◇◇

The ringing of the telephone jarred me to my feet,
"Who," I thought with anger, *"is arousing me from sleep?"*
For glancing at the clock that sat beside my bed,
I noted now the time, half-past six, it read.
"Hello," I said quite sharply, as I spoke into the phone.
"Oh, Pastor," came the shaky voice,
      "I'm glad that you are home."
"You see," the woman quickly said, with a raspy, broken cry,
"my brother, Dan O'Reilly, in the early morning, died."
"Died?" I muttered hoarsely, from shock and disbelief.
"Yes," she said, and cried aloud with bitter pain and grief.
"They called it hypothermia; exposure to the cold."
"Oh, Pastor," she now moaned, fighting for control,
"would you come and help me in this awful Hour of Need?"
"Why, yes, my dear," I answered her,
      "I'll be there . . . certainly!"

And then still stunned, I slowly turned,
      replacing now the phone;
wondering what had happened once
      my good friend reached his home.
Oh, yes, he wasn't feeling well . . . that I clearly saw,
but then I, too, had battled, once, a torrential rainfall!
And after fiercely grappling with that violent storm at sea,
I had had no more than just a mild cold for a week! . . .

"Oh," I cried out brokenly, with deep-felt hurt and pain,
"why did that old useless car break down in the rain?"

And then a verse of Scripture, crossed my troubled mind;
offering me a solace in this horrid, painful time . . .
"Comfort, ye, My people," God's Holy Word did say,
and in my heart, I truly knew, those words I had obeyed.
For as his life was fleeting from off this earthly sphere,
words of warmth and comfort, from my own lips, Dan did hear!
And so I prayed and thanked the Lord for allowing me
to counsel with my dear, good friend
      in his final Hour of Need . . .
And thinking of his wretched car, I once more shook my head
o'er the life it cost my friend . . ."*Poor 'ol Dan,"* I said.

WHOSOEVER

*Color me blue, yellow and red;
glimpse my heart, of evil repent.*

" . . . He [the King] did much evil in the sight of the LORD, provoking Him to anger."

II Chronicles 33: 6b

"For God so loved the world, that He gave His only begotten Son, that whosoever believeth in Him should not perish, but have everlasting life."

John 3: 16 (KJV)

The fire burned brightly on the mountain-top that night
as slowly, ritualistically, the High Priest plunged his knife
into the thin, limp body of the quivering little child,
bound upon the altar of the goddess, dark and vile. . . .
Blood poured off that altar of putrid sacrifice
as the King now chanted words; the goddess to entice
and bodies, hard and sensual, swayed in bloodied form,
embracing one another; lustful acts performed. . . .

Oh, how the King took pleasure in such wanton evil deeds,
delighting in the altars built and followers to lead
into vile debauchery in this arrant, pagan land;
conforming to the worship the goddess did demand! . . .
Oh, how the King did revel in the people he now led
off the bloodied mountain-top . . . to their homes, again;
confident that worshiping the dark and evil lords
guaranteed his people protection, evermore;
confident that his own land, in safety, now did rest
from the pagan, warring tribes that 'round his country lived;
confident disaster would never touch his throne,
as their fearful, pagan gods, became his very own!

But God, in his great Heaven, was raising up a foe;
a nation cruel and mighty, the king to overthrow. . . .
And suddenly his Kingdom, by force, came crashing down
and the wicked King was dragged . . .
      by chains . . . to prison, bound!
There within the stillness of a hellish, putrid tomb,
the King recounted, in his mind, the evils he'd pursued. . . .
Divination, sorceries, topped his lengthy list;
defilement of God's Temple; blasphemous contempt!
Witchcraft . . . vile devotion to abhorrent, pagan gods;
forcing his own sons, the fiery flames to trod! . . .

Sacrificing forth their lives; the gods to e'er appease;
in vile and evil worship, his subjects he would lead,
teaching them to follow his actions and his words;
atrocious human evil . . . on icy cold altars! . . .
Altars magnifying a dark and venomous force;
necromancy and murder; his life's despicable course!
Oh, the horrid evils this King did magnify! . . .
Oh, the lives polluted; contamination's blight! . . .
Oh, the judgment brought upon his subjects, one and all,
as evil was exalted . . . replacing God's own Laws!

◇◇◇◇◇◇◇

But now within his prison cell, in silence, all alone
he came before the Righteous Judge . . .
      and bowed before His Throne.
And greatly did he humble, himself, before the LORD;
crying o'er the evils, vile, his heart in anguish bore! . . .
And suddenly God's mercy touched his throbbing soul;
forgiveness to impart; love to make him whole! . . .
Suddenly this sinner; this evil, wretched King
found himself forgiven . . . a new life to begin! . . .
Suddenly he realized that God, Who reigns on High,
is the LORD of all; the One e'er magnified!

Yes, God restored this wicked King, once more,
      to his own throne;
forgiving him for all his evil deeds, in darkness sown;
loving him as much as He now loves both you and me,
showing him compassion . . . his prisoned soul to free! . . .
And this great King, God once more placed within Jerusalem,
where he glorified the LORD until his reign was done!

Manasseh—such an evil King . . . far more than all the rest;
and yet a man that God redeemed through humbled brokenness!
A man who knew the depths of sin; depravity so vile
became, at last, a man of God . . . by love e'er reconciled!

Manasseh—God's reminder, for men of every age,
that *"whosoever will may come"* . . . God's love is just that great!

The Bible says . . .

"Manasseh . . . did evil in the sight of the LORD according to the abominations of the nations whom the LORD dispossessed before the sons of Israel. For he rebuilt the high places . . . he also erected altars for the Baals . . . he built altars in the House of the LORD . . . he made his sons pass through the fire in the valley of Ben-hinnom; and he practiced witchcraft, used divination, practiced sorcery, and dealt with mediums and spiritists. He did much evil in the sight of the LORD, provoking Him to anger . . . Manasseh misled Judah and the inhabitants of Jerusalem to do more evil than the nations whom the LORD destroyed before the sons of Israel. And the LORD spoke to Manasseh and his people, but they paid no attention. Therefore the LORD brought the commanders of the army of the King of Assyria against them, and they captured Manasseh with hooks, [put through the nose], bound him with bronze chains, and took him to Babylon.

And when he was in distress, he entreated the LORD his God and humbled himself greatly before the God of his fathers. When he prayed to Him, He was moved by his entreaty and heard his supplication, and brought him again to Jerusalem, to his kingdom. Then Manasseh knew that the LORD was God.

Now after this ... he ... removed the foreign gods and the idol from the House of the LORD, as well as all the altars which he had built on the mountain of the House of the LORD and in Jerusalem, and he threw them outside the City. And he set up the altar of the LORD and sacrificed peace offerings and thank offerings on it; and he ordered Judah to serve the LORD God of Israel."

II Chronicles 33: 1–2, 3–4, 6, 9–13, 14, 15–16

"If Thou, LORD, shouldst mark inquities, O Lord, who could stand? But there is forgiveness with Thee, that Thou mayest be feared.... For with the LORD there is lovingkindness, and with Him is abundant redemption."

Psalm 130: 3–4, 7b

Contact Darla O'Neill
or order more copies of this book at

TATE PUBLISHING, LLC

127 East Trade Center Terrace
Mustang, Oklahoma 73064

(888) 361 - 9473

Tate Publishing, LLC

www.tatepublishing.com